Biking for Grownups

Margaret Bennett

BIKING FOR GROWNUPS

Illustrated with drawings

DODD, MEAD & COMPANY
New York

FOR LARRY AND BOBBIE BRANSON—

If people were made out of bicycle
components, they would be total Campy.

Library of Congress Cataloging in Publication Data

Bennett, Margaret, fl. 1967–
    Biking for grownups.

    Bibliography: p.
    Includes index.
    1. Cycling. I. Title.
GV1041.B44   796.6   75-42499
ISBN 0-396-07288-7

CONTENTS

chapter **I**

THE BEST OF ALL
POSSIBLE SPORTS

I assume that if you're reading this book you have
at least a spark of interest in biking or maybe even
the flame of enthusiasm. What I want to do is fan that
spark or flame into a conflagration. You may already
think biking is good, but you probably don't fully realize how magnificently wonderful it is in how many
different ways.

LIFE CYCLE: Where I live in the high desert country
of Southern California there is a man I see every day
methodically pedaling around and around the block
on a three-wheel bike. He is grim and gray-faced, obviously riding a prescribed number of circuits on his

1

doctor's orders to aid in recuperation from a heart attack or stroke. How sad to have to bike for recovery. If he had biked for fun, he possibly never would have had his near-fatal heart attack to recover from.

Biking—*regular* biking—is one of the very best defense weapons against cardiovascular problems, those civilization-induced ailments 55 percent of us die from. Not only does the constant rhythmic leg movement squeeze the blood vessels and pump the blood more efficiently from those far-off extremities to the heart, it actually builds up an additional system of blood vessels. This is called collateral circulation. This increased number of blood vessels can save your life in times of stress. In addition, regular bicycling gradually increases the heart's volume. When you stop to consider how much trouble is caused, especially in later years, by a narrowing of blood vessels and a decrease in heart volume, you can see what superb preventive maintenance biking can be.

Biking is a great aerobic exercise. The best description I've heard of what an aerobic exercise is and does was made by eighty-four-year-old cyclist Clarence Picard, who recently did the annual 460-mile 6-day Iowa cross-state bike trip. He said, "Older people should take some kind of exercise three times a week or more often that will bring the heart up to its full extension of effort. You want the heart to beat hard, but not for very long, so that it can get used to meeting emergencies like catching a streetcar or heading off a hog."

Steady, regular biking can also reduce hypertension (high blood pressure) sometimes to the extent that those on medication can stop taking it. Biking can even keep the liver from developing fatty deposits, which can lead to cirrhosis, and it can keep the wolf of bone deterioration at bay. All this without a prescription or a drug hangover or harmful side effects.

THE WEIGHTING GAME: A bicycle is a great reducing machine. If you keep everything else equal and add cycling, you automatically subtract pounds. Statistically a 165-pound person has to bike 73 miles at 9½ miles per hour to burn off one pound, but it seems to work out better than that in practice. This may be because, contrary to the myth that the more you exercise the more you eat, you actually often eat less. Nutritionist Jean Mayer of Harvard found in his studies that people who just sit around collecting fat generally eat more than those who exercise regularly. Dr. Al Marston, appearing on the television special, "It's a Matter of Fat," takes the theory one step further, saying, "You've got to keep moving to keep that appetite down. It's paradoxical, but it's true."

Not only does biking help you lose weight, it helps you lose it in a more attractive way. A study of reducing women made at Kent State University showed that those who lost weight by exercise alone or by diet plus exercise developed more attractive figures than those who just dieted. I don't know how they made the rather subjective "more attractive" analysis, but it does stand to reason that the firmness of thigh muscle and slenderness of ankle developed from an exercise like biking beat the sometimes gaunt, stringy appearance dieting alone can cause.

TWO-WHEEL LIBRIUM: A British medical team headed by Dr. Malcolm Carruthers recently came up with the dumbfounding finding that there is a hormone called norepinephrine that makes you feel happy. How do we get a joy pop of this hormone? We exercise for it. Dr. Carruthers discovered that only ten minutes of suitable exercise doubles the body's level of norepinephrine.

This is one hunk of medical research I can believe in. I know from experience that a bike ride releases some kind of good juice within. You invariably begin feeling that life is not as bad as it seemed before you started out, that your problems are not insurmountable, after all, that the tight screw in the back of your neck has been loosened by some benevolent force. Somehow getting on a bike and pedaling off under your own power makes you think, however erroneously, that you have control over your destiny, that you are a free agent.

This feeling of control doesn't come from the happy hormone alone. Some of it comes from plain old oxygen. It is a scientific fact that the blood vessel squeezing caused by constant pedaling makes the blood circulate faster and therefore shoots more oxygen to the brain. You can actually think better after you've been on a bike for a while, and you do have more problem-solving ability.

Riding in tandem with these sensations of control are feelings of freedom. A good part of this freedom, I believe, comes from getting away from all your possessive and oppressive possessions. As Kazantakas wrote for his epitaph, "I have nothing . . . I fear nothing . . . I am free." It's just you and the simple machine and maybe a small bag with a few basic tools and a lunch. You're not dependent on anybody for anything—at least, for a while. After a day of such freedom feelings you can return home and stick your head back through the yoke, secure in the knowledge that you can slip it out again and escape on your bike anytime you want to.

For my money—or maybe that should be for my lack of money—a day on the bike is worth a year on the couch.

chapter 2

WHAT IS A BIKE?

IN CYCLO VERITAS: Bicycles and wine have a lot in common. Both are aesthetically and sensually pleasing—the wine with its glowing, living color, its rich bouquet and the "peacock's tail" of flavors it spreads upon your tongue; the bike with its shining paint and glittering chrome and the tactile and kinesthetic delights you experience when you're clicking along at one with it. Both wine and bikes, if you don't overdo with them, leave you with a warm glow and a feeling of well-being.

Once you're introduced to either of these two pleasures, you begin to have a desire to become a connoisseur. Your taste refines with knowledge. Where once you could be happy with a screw top jug of wine and a balloon-tired clunker, you find yourself longing to put your nose to a Romanée Conti or a Chateau Lafite Rothschild and your seat to the saddle of a Colnago or a Hetchings.

Financially speaking, bikes are again like wines. You inevitably get what you pay for. There are very few bargains. Then, too, once you reach a certain level of quality in either, it begins to take a great deal of money to effect a very small degree of improvement.

Another great degree of similarity lies in the attitude of the aficionados. It is sad but true that a number of wine experts and bike experts develop into rather unpleasant snobs who seem to get more of their kicks from putting down the less knowledgeable than from their passion for the activity itself. ("You mean you actually drank a Moselle with beef Wellington?!" "You mean you actually put touring handlebars and a basket on a Masi?!")

But happily the number one similarity between bikes and wines is that they each have one major and overriding purpose: to give pleasure. And nobody can tell you what is most pleasurable to you except yourself. Naturally, you have to experiment to see what you like—taste a number of wines, try out a number of different bikes and components. And you have to read and ask questions and learn about both, because admittedly there's a lot to know on both subjects. Still, in the case of both wines and biking, it all boils down finally to one thing: individual preference.

Here, then, I'll tell you all the "expert" opinion on bicycles and bicycling—often diametrically opposed expert opinion—and I'll also tell you what, as they say in mountain country, pleasures me. Then you can find your own formula—as unique as your fingerprints—for maximum cycling enjoyment

A Bicycle Built for You

Despite the fact that the bike is a basic and basically simple vehicle, there are almost endless variations on the two-wheel theme. As grownups, we'll eliminate right off the banana-seated high risers with and without motocross variations that the sub-adults favor. We'll also not go into the more esoteric unicycles, tandems and currently-being-revived large front-wheeled boneshakers of yore. These are the styles of locomotion you might want to get involved with after you've mastered the basics, rather in the way that a painter goes abstract after he's learned how to draw fingers and apples.

We'll also rend your nostalgic heart by eliminating the balloon-tired one-speed coaster brake model of your golden childhood memories. These are just too heavy and too clumsy to make cycling enjoyable.

And finally we'll put at least a semi-kibosh on folding bikes. Their seeming advantage of easy storage and easy totability is outweighed, appropriately enough, by greater weight, as well as less stability and riding ease, because of their small wheels and the fact that the best they offer in gears is a three-speed.

All this elimination leaves us with the basic two for the road: the 3-speed and the 10-speed.

SPEED LIMIT: The 3-speed is sometimes called an English racer, a term which vastly amuses knowledgeable cyclists, because this bike is not necessarily English (although an English firm, Raleigh, makes some of the best) and it most definitely is not a racer. Racing with a 3-speed would be like entering a pickup truck at Le Mans.

Three-speeds usually weigh around 37 pounds. They also usually have the flat touring handlebars rather than the underslung variety. The saddles are the wider, softer mattress kind rather than the hard, slim, springless racing type.

The 3-speed has some advantages. There's much less to go wrong and get out of adjustment than on the more sensitive, highly tuned 10-speed. The gears are protected inside the hub, where fate and accidents cannot harm them. It's easier to shift a 3-speed, too. You just stop pedaling and move the level on the handlebars to one of the three numbers and, click, you're in a new gear.

Three-speeds are much less expensive than 10-speeds. You can get a topnotch 3-speed for about $100, while a first-rate 10-speed will set you back at least quadruple that price.

There are many fine testimonials to 3-speeds by people who would ride nothing else, have taken them all over the world, including, to hear them tell it, up the steep side of the Matterhorn. Three-speed fanatics in fits of reverse snobbism enjoy ranting that 10-speeds are nothing but effete status machines designed by greedy manufacturers to bilk the naive public out of numerous dollars. Three-speed freaks are entitled to their opinion, and since I've been so generous in allowing them theirs, I will now allow myself mine. I think the only reason you would like riding a 3-speed would be that you had only ridden a 1-speed before—and it is admittedly a huge improvement over that—and you had not yet ridden a 10-speed.

I happily rode a 3-speed for years. I even upgraded my lesser 3-speed to a beautiful Raleigh, elegant in a Mercedes brown coat, natty little leather tool kit dangling from the back of a Brooks saddle. I thought I had achieved the ultimate in cycling. Then I bit the 10-speed fruit and 3-speed biking was paradise lost. I didn't know it was lost at the time. I just temporarily put my 3-speed aside while I got myself used to the complexities of 10-speed shifting.

I kept the 3-speed with the idea that because of its basket and its nice solid, dependable character I could use it for shopping and trips to the post office and other such utilitarian activities. It sat in the garage covered with a plastic sheet for about six months. I kept *intending* to use it, but somehow the 10-speed was always gassed up and ready to go.

Then it came to pass that my 10-speed was in the shop getting bent back into shape after being involved in an airline shipping demolition project. Since a day without a bike ride is like an orange juice commercial without Anita Bryant, I whisked off the plastic sheet, leapt aboard my 3-speed and pedaled off. No, better make that plodded off.

The long flat desert roads around my home now seemed like paths up the Andes. I felt my feet were in diving boots and my legs, which were in Presidential-Sports-Award shape, seemed as weak as if they had just emerged from six months in casts and traction. I hyperbolize, of course, but the inescapable truth was that biking had suddenly turned from soaring joy to plain grim work. My 3-speed is now sitting in my local bike shop waiting to be sold on consignment. That's proof of my strength of conviction that a 10-speed is the only way to fly on a bicycle.

Incidentally, 5-speeds and 15-speeds are merely variations on the 10-speed theme. I don't see much reason for the former. It's little if any less expensive, the five gears don't lift you very far out of the confining realm of the 3-speed, and you still have to learn to shift the back derailleur. The 15-speed is slightly heavier than a 10-speed and in certain of its gears the chain likes to drag. But if you do a lot of touring on varied terrain, a 15-speed is worth considering. (It's very easy to convert a 10-speed to a 15-speed.)

Since the 10-speed is the basic pleasure package you'll be buying, let's break it down now for inspection or, better still, let's build it up.

Anatomy of a 10-speed Bicycle

FRAME: The frame is make up of:

head tube	seat stays
top tube	chain stays
down tube	bottom bracket (hanger)
seat tube	drop-outs

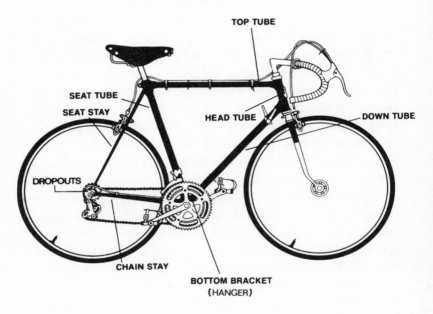

Many bicycle manufacturers make the frame only and buy from suppliers all the components, that is to say, everything else that goes on the frame to make a bicycle into a bicycle. They assemble the total product, slap on their decal, and, *voilá*, they have manufactured a bicycle. Some bicycle manufacturers actually make nothing at all. They design the frame and send off the specs to a frame maker. But however they handle it, they all start the building of a bicycle with a frame.

THE FRAME IN THE PICTURE: Aside from the newly developed space age titanium frames, which are super-light, super-strong and super-expensive (around $450), most bicycles have steel frames. But steel frames are no more alike than are human flesh and bone bodies. In the old Sears, Roebuck catalogs they used to categorize their merchandise as good, better and best. We can follow a similar pattern with bike frames, except the bottom category must be more frankly termed poor instead of good.

Poor: On a bike costing under $100 the frame is likely to be made of what I've heard racers scornfully call "water pipe." It isn't really water pipe, of course, but it might be a little better suited to carrying water than to being the heart of a bike. It is heavy, weak and unresponsive, and a heavy, weak-hearted unresponsive bike is exactly what you don't want.

The tubes of poor frames are made from flat sheets which are wrapped around rollers to shape them. They are then welded. These tubes with welded seams are weak, because the heat of the welding process alters the crystal structure of the metal, making it more susceptible to fatigue. To refresh yourself as to what happens in metal fatigue, open up a paper clip and bend it back and forth a few times. Metal fatigue is also what happened to the Comet airplanes that were popping passengers out the windows and into the Mediterranean a few years back. And metal fatigue is what can eventually break down a bike frame of the poor category.

As if the weakness of the tubing weren't enough, the joints, where most of the stress is, are also welded. The joints are thus susceptible to the same metal fatigue as the tubes themselves, only more so. Admittedly, this type of frame probably won't fall apart under normal civilized adult use, but it definitely does not inspire feelings of confidence.

Better: When you move up into the $100-$200-bike category, the frame lightens and strengthens and becomes more ridable, because a higher quality steel alloy is used and the tubes are seamless. They're made by hollowing out solid ingots and, therefore, do not have welded seams.

In this price range the tubes are further strengthened by being joined together, not by welding, but by brazing. Metal sleeves, called lugs, are used at the joints in conjunction with brazing. Brazing is a process in which two pieces of metal to be joined, in this case the tube and the lug, are heated and then fastened together with molten brass or silver alloy. The brass or silver flows into the metal of the tube and lug by capillary action. (If you want to see capillary action in action, dip one end of a sugar cube into a cup of coffee.) Brazing weakens the structure of the metal only slightly, because the metal is not heated to as high a temperature as is necessary in welding. Silver brazing alloys require less heat than brass alloys, but are much more expensive. Some quality bikes are brazed without the use of lugs—the Ferrare Super Chrome, for instance—but most people prefer the looks of lugged frames.

Best: In the over-$200 bikes you usually get frames of the lightest and strongest of steel alloys—manganese molybdenum or chrome molybdenum. The British-made Reynolds 531 alloy (they say five-three-one rather than five thirty-one) is used so much and advertised so heavily that you get the idea it's the only girl in town. Not so. In the same top category are Columbus and Falck (Italian), Vitus (French), Mansmann (German), and Day and Day (Japanese). In fact, each of these alloy steels has its fans who consider it best. Columbus is particularly popular with racers because of its greater stiffness and with bike manufacturers because of the different grades of stiffness available. The Japanese Chromeloy is good and there is also American Chrome Molybdenum.

The lugs used on the best frames are also the best, usually made by Nervex, Prugnat or Bocama. I present these lug names purely for academic interest and so that in case some name-dropper drops them all over you, you'll know what he's talking about. Unless you're a bike frame builder, you probably won't be able to tell one lug maker's product from another; don't lose any sleep over that. Suffice it to say that a bike built with top tubing is going to be joined with top lugs. These sometimes are more rococo and ornate with many a curve and cutaway to make them lighter and to give a greater area of contact with the tube and distribute the stress better. They are tapered down so that they're thin where they meet the tube and are often artistically handlined with a different colored paint just inside the edge.

The very best frames have other significant but invisible features. The tubes are butted. This means they are slightly thickened at the ends. Butting gives tubes added strength where they're joined and most likely to break and allows them to be thinner in the middle where not so much strength is required. The tubes are also mitered. That is to say, they are cut to fit together at the joints. They are not just shoved up against each other and, in effect, held in place by the lug.

Without X-ray eyes, how are you to know that these over-$200 bikes are indeed made with the best of all possible steels and butted tubes? Fortunately, it's easy. Just as no Frenchman awarded the Legion of Honor would be caught dead without the signifying red ribbon on his lapel, any bike frame made with one of the big-name alloy steels and butted tubes is going to wear the decal that says so. (Distress note: In one bike shop I saw Reynolds decals for sale. These ostensibly were for people whose decals had fallen off or gotten scratched off their bikes. But as a psychologist friend of mine always says, "The ostensible is never the real.") If a frame is handmade and expensive, you just plain have to believe that it's mitered. Some things have to be taken on faith and this is one of them.

JUST ANOTHER PRETTY FRAME: To the untrained eye all bike frames look alike. So how can you tell a good frame from a not-so-good one? You've got to get your eye in training by looking at lots and lots of frames— the poor as well as the best and all those in between. An architect friend of mine insists that it's just as important to look at bad furniture as it is to look at good. So it is with frames. Look carefully at bikes in each of the price categories and soon you'll be able to tell quality without even looking at the price tag.

Of course, even within each category there are good jobs and mediocre jobs in supposedly identical bikes. You'll become more aware of this the more you look. For example, a good job of brazing has no bits of brass or silver showing where the worker let it dribble out and didn't file it off. Neither are there empty spaces between the lug and the tube—spaces large enough to let you insert your fingernail. Even the paint jobs can have great variations, which, after you've looked at a certain number, will shriek of quality or carelessness.

And one final telling point about judging frames. No matter how many you look at, there is only one true determination of a frame's quality. This ultimate definition of a good bike frame is, in the words of a leading bicycle manufacturer: "If it doesn't break down, it's a good bike frame."

FORK ASSEMBLY: The fork assembly is made up of:

stem	headset
handlebars	fork

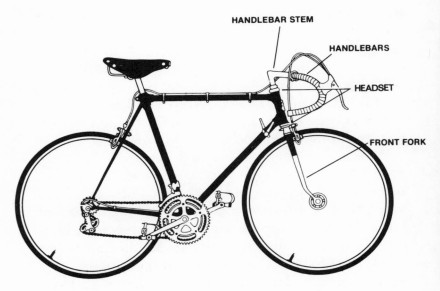

HANDLEBAR STEM

HANDLEBARS

HEADSET

FRONT FORK

The stem and handlebars are made of steel in the lesser breeds of bike and of lighter aluminum alloy in the better. The best bikes have stems with a recessed bolt, which makes for a more handsome appearance and a bit more safety.

With handlebars we're faced with two main styles

and infinite variations within each style. We're all familiar with the shape of drop bars and the shape of flat bars, but here are the three basic designs for each:

Drop bars:

PISTA   MAES   RANDONNEUR

Flat bars (top view):

Incidentally, handlebar terminology has lots of variation, too. The drops are known as racing, underslung, turned-down, hooked, butterfly, and goats' horns. The flats can be called sport, all rounder, high, upright, porter and in Britishese comfort bars. Drop bars are taped with cloth or plastic, while rubber or plastic grips are used with flat handlebars.

The headset is an important part of the bike and hence an important part to have of good quality. It is responsible both for holding the fork on securely and for smooth turning. The headset is a component of many parts. In the galloping cheapies this is one of the places where you can find plastic instead of steel bearings. Even bikes up a notch or so from the bottom category can have cracks or worn spots or generally imprecise fitting so that when you turn the handlebars, there is a scraping and dragging. (Avoid a bike that does this, because it's a condition that doesn't go away. It only gets worse.)

In the top bikes you'll find headsets made by Zeus, Stronglite, and Campagnolo. With any of these you're as sure as possible to get everything a headset should be.

The fork is another part of the bike which in the better models is made of a topnotch seamless chrome molybdenum tubing with all the resultant strength, resiliency and lightness. Many of the top bikes have chrome on the forks, which makes for good looks and good looks that last. The forks, incidentally, are tapered to give strength at the top and resiliency at the ends. This design provides a safe and smooth ride. The curve of the fork (the rake) influences the stiffness of the ride.

The fork tips, which hold the axle of the front wheel, and the drop-outs, which do the same job for the rear wheel, are stamped out and welded on in the cheaper bikes with all the weaknesses of these two processes. On the better bikes the fork tips and drop-outs are forged and brazed for strength and long life.

BOTTOM BRACKET: The bottom bracket is made up of:

> hanger
> bottom bracket assembly
> crankset

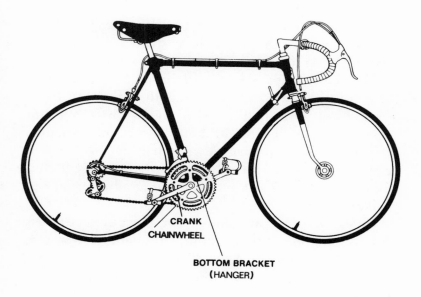

CRANK
CHAINWHEEL

BOTTOM BRACKET
(HANGER)

The hanger is where the down tube, the seat tube and the chain stays all meet. It's the small tube into which fits the bottom bracket assembly. The assembly is really the bicycle's engine. It's composed of an axle, bearings, and cups to contain the bearings.

The crankset is the two chainwheels plus the two cranks or arms that rotate when you pedal. Each arm fits into the bottom bracket assembly on one end and has a pedal attached at the other. The poorest crank-sets are made in one piece of forged steel and will often be found on the under-$100 bikes. Better is the cottered crank. This is made of steel, and the bottom bracket assembly and cranks are separate entities, joined with a cotter pin. These pins are easy to see when you're checking out bikes, since they stick out like a sore thumb on one side of the crank, and the nut and washer that hold them stick out even more obviously on the other.

The best bikes come with aluminum-alloy cotterless cranks, which have a smooth visage, are lightweight, are less likely to slip under stress, and are easier to maintain, should do-it-yourself maintenance turn out to be your bag. A prejudice you will notice emerging is mine for alloy cotterless cranks. I find them one of the most significant upgradings you can make on a bike.

Good and recommended brands of cotterless cranks include Campagnolo, Shimano Dura-Ace, Stronglite, Sugino, T.A., and Zeus.

And here's a tip for those among you who know that do-it-yourself maintenance is *not* going to be your bag. Phil Wood makes a sealed crank bearing that does not need to be lubed for five glorious years. It can be used on any bike regardless of its race, creed or country of origin. It can be ordered with mounting rings to fit either Italian, British, French, or Swiss bottom bracket threading.

PEDALS: On lightweight bikes, nonracing style, pedals are usually rattrap design. This means they are all metal and serrated. The better ones weigh only about 10 ounces and can be taken apart for lubrication. A quality pedal is a good investment, but it is a whopper of an investment. Campagnolos are now going for over $60.

The cheaper pedals are rubber and very heavy, but they do have one saving feature. Your foot doesn't slip off them as easily as off metal.

BRAKES: Brakes on 10-speeds are ordinarily the caliper type with levers located on the handlebars. When you squeeze the levers in toward the handlebars, rubber brake shoes press against the wheel rims and provide stopping action. The left lever generally controls the front wheel brake and the right one the rear wheel brake. (But be sure to check!)

There are two basic designs for caliper brakes—centerpull and sidepull. Most of the medium-priced 10-speeds come equipped with centerpulls. Mafac and Universal and Weinmann are the outstanding brand names. Centerpull fans claim these stay in adjustment better—in fact, are somewhat self-adjusting—and brake more evenly than sidepulls.

Sidepulls are found on the least expensive (they're less costly to manufacture) and on the most expensive bikes. This odd situation is explained by the fact that there's a Grand Canyon of difference between really good sidepulls and the not-so-good ones. On the superior ones you'll see the name Campagnolo, Shimano Dura-Ace, Grand Compe, or Weinmann 500.

Sidepull fanciers believe sidepulls have more positive action; you can stop faster. They claim sidepulls
stay in adjustment longer, because the cable does not
stretch so readily. The only point on which sidepull
fanciers make a concession is to agree that centerpulls work better when they're out of adjustment
than sidepulls do when *they're* out of adjustment

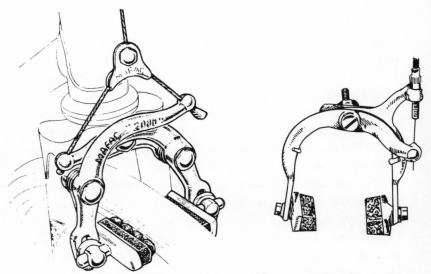

*Left: Centerpull caliper brakes. Right: Sidepull caliper
brakes.*

(some concession there!). This controversy can be
definitively resolved by putting the new Shimano
"Auto-Adjust" brakes on your bicycle. These sidepulls *do* stay in adjustment longer, because they have
a one-way clutch that automatically regulates the tension as you ride.

Another innovation Shimano has introduced is a disc brake which can be operated either with cables or hydraulically. It performs beautifully and safely in all weather conditions, and will outdo any other kind of brake in wet weather. Now here are the rubs. Disc brakes need heavy seat stays, they require a shallow flange width (meaning the round fitting on the hub to which the spokes attach is narrow), and unless you use extra heavy spokes with them, you may find you've become a great spoke snapper. But the worst feature of discs at the moment is that they're terribly heavy and therefore used mainly on bikes for rough-and-ready teen-agers.

HUBS: Hubs are a place where strength and precise operation count for much, since they have bearings and are load bearing. The lesser bikes have steel hubs. These are strong but heavy. The better bikes go for the lighter aluminum alloy and are usually quick release. This means they have a little lever you can flip to drop out your wheel in an instant for tire repair or hauling in the trunk of your car or storing or what-you-will.

Excellent quick release alloy hubs are made by Campagnolo, Shimano Dura-Ace, Sanshin, Triplex, Normandy, and Zeus. But my favorites are the Hi-E and the Phil Wood. I like them because, like the Phil Wood crank bearing, they are sealed so that the cruds of the road cannot get in. As a result they need no maintenance for three years in the case of Hi-E and with Phil Wood you get his customary five glorious years of freedom from disassembling and regreasing. (You also get his glorious price of over $50 for the two hubs.) This no-maintenance feature may have more significance for you when you stop to consider that under active use the ordinary hub needs maintenance about every six months.

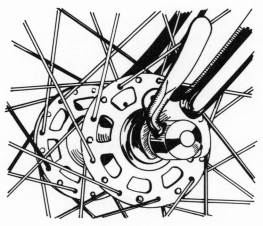

Quick release hub

Low flange hubs are more comfortable for riding and high flange hubs give greater strength and stability, especially in hill climbing.

WHEELS: With wheels, too, it's a question of steel for cheaper bikes and aluminum alloy for the better ones. The exception is that bicyclists who have a perverted taste for tremendously rough roads or potholed terrain might use steel rims for durability, even on a better bike. Since wheels are low-down and moving—in fact, you can hardly get more low-down and moving than they are—the lightness of the alloy makes a big difference in performance.

Good spokes are often doubled-butted just like frames for strength and lightness.

You will need different wheel rims depending on what kind of tires you use. Some rims are dimpled the better for the brake blocks to grab. Some say this kind of rim, however, wears the brake blocks excessively and gives poorer stopping power in wet weather when the dimples fill up with water.

TIRES: A tire is a tire is a tire, right? No. There are some obvious and subtle differences. The most obvious difference is between clinchers, which are used on most lower- and middle-priced bikes, and sew-ups (also called tubulars just to confuse, because clinchers have tubes, too), which are usually put on the best bikes. We'll discuss the merits and de of the different tires later in Chapter 4. For right now, okay, a tire is a tire is a tire.

GEARS: The gears are made up of:

chainwheel	front derailleur
chain	rear derailleur
freewheel	shifting levers

The chainwheel on 10-speeds consists of two sprockets of different sizes. Each is ringed with teeth to engage the chain and thereby transmit your pedal power to the back wheel. In a 15-speed bike there are three sprockets on the chainwheel; in a 5-speed only one.

The chainwheel usually comes with the cranks, and the quality you get in the one is the same as in the other.

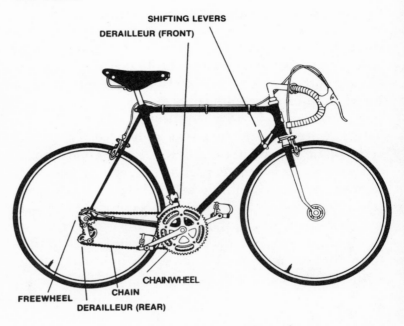

SHIFTING LEVERS
DERAILLEUR (FRONT)
CHAINWHEEL
CHAIN
FREEWHEEL
DERAILLEUR (REAR)

A chain is a chain is a chain, although you can pay more and get one finished in gold color.

The freewheel is a set of five sprockets of different sizes next to the hub of the rear wheel. Quality in the freewheel is not as significant as the number of teeth in each sprocket. This determines your gear ratios. We'll discuss these in Chapter 4.

Derailleurs are small cages which enclose the chain and move it from one sprocket to another. There are two derailleurs on a 10-speed—a front derailleur and a rear one. The shifting lever on the left controls the front derailleur. The one on the right moves the rear derailleur.

Derailleurs are connected to the shifting levers by wire cables. When you move a lever, the cable causes the derailleur to change position, taking the chain along with it. The chain is "derailed" from one sprocket and switched to the next.

With derailleurs, quality and cost again rear their heads. And again the alloy ones are better and lighter. The major companies, Campagnolo, Shimano, Huret, Simplex, Sun Tour, Zeus, etc., make derailleurs in both steel and alloy. The brand name is not as important as the material used. Better a Shimano alloy than a Campagnolo steel. The better quality derailleurs are not just lighter. They also shift more decisively and precisely.

Shifting levers are most commonly located on the down tube. Sometimes they come on the stem behind the handlebars, where they may be a bit more convenient, but they could be a hazard in an accident and they don't function quite as well. A third and increasingly popular location for shifters is on the ends of the handlebars.

SEAT POSTS AND SADDLES: There are different qualities in seat posts as in everything. Aluminum alloy is

more expensive and lighter; steel is less expensive
and heavier, as in all bike components.

The saddles we'll discuss in Chapter 4.

Whew! And that, finally, is a bicycle.

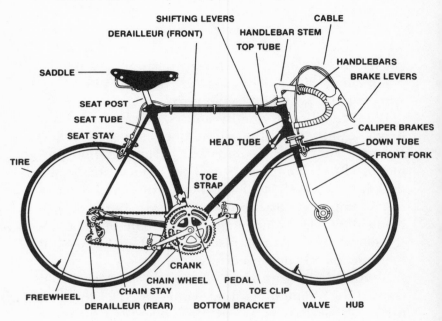

chapter 3

IN THE MARKET
FOR A BIKE

SHOP TALK: In Los Angeles there used to be a TV show called "Cavalcade of Books." On this program learned ladies and gentlemen reviewed the latest books with such intellectual lip-smacking that you wanted to rush right out and get them all. At the end of the show there was always an answer period for questions sent in by viewers. The one question I remember was, "I *so* enjoy your program and I would *love* to read the books you recommend, but my question is this: Where can I buy all these wonderful books?"

One panel member pondered, focused on the camera and announced portentously, "I would suggest you buy them in a bookstore."

It may seem the same sort of flogging of the obvious to suggest that you buy your bike in a bicycle shop, but it isn't really. The temptation to buy elsewhere is all around you. Inexpensive bicycles clog the aisles of discount houses, department stores, toy shops, variety stores, hardware stores and even drugstores. They're all lined up there shiny of paint and glittering of chrome. A great truth about bicycles is that *any* new bike looks good, even downright beautiful. But that beauty is only paint and chrome deep, and on a cheap bike the paint and chrome aren't all that deep.

THE QUALITY IS STRAINED: The reason the prices are low in discount houses—often around $50 less than a "similar" bike in a bike shop—is that the quality is most often low, too. The frame and components are cheap and flimsy, both in terms of material and construction.

Most of the discount cheapie bikes come from Taiwan. Now while I don't want a Taiwan tong to put a contract on me for my remarks, I have to state that at this moment in manufacturing, Taiwan bikes tend to be junkers. For one thing they often have plastic bearings, which last for about three months, if you're lucky. For another, well, laconic Larry Branson, my local bike shop oracle, pretty much summed it up when I asked him exactly what's wrong with Taiwan bikes. He thought a minute and said, "I can't think of anything that's *right* with them."

It's not always easy to tell a Taiwan bike. Many of them have a pretty good cover. They may be emblazoned with medallions and splashed with decals that proclaim them to be "custom made" for the discount house vending them. They may have names more British-sounding than Winston Churchill. They may even have " made in Germany" stamped on them. This is not a total deception. What's made in Germany is the steel. The turning of that steel into a poor-quality bike frame took place in a Taiwan back street.

One bike shop owner told me that about half his repair business consists of trying to put discount house bikes in usable condition. This can cost the bike owner up to $40. When you add that to the purchase price, "the bargain" begins to look like the expensive proposition that it is. On top of that, even when the bike is fixed up, all you really have is a fixed-up crummy bike.

GETTING IT TOGETHER: Now let's say you're certain the bike on sale at the discount house or department store is a quality bike, because it's manufactured by a well-known company that turns out nothing but quality products. Let's say they happen to have your frame size—not likely unless you are the prototype of Mr. Averageman or Ms. Averagewoman. Can you then assume that you're perfectly safe in buying the bike? Nope. With bikes it's not simply a matter of a reliable brand name. Bikes are shipped to dealers in a box approximately 3' x 6' x 7". Somebody has to do the final assembly. That means they have to attach the seat, handlebars, pedals, adjust the brakes and derailleurs and make sure all the nuts and bolts and screws are where they should be and are tight. The quality of the assembly is as important to you as the quality of what's inside the box.

In a bike shop it's more likely than not that an experienced, trained and knowledgeable bike mechanic will be the assembler. In one of the other kinds of dispensaries you run the risk of having your bike put together by a stock boy, an idle sales clerk, or maybe a few teen-agers who want to earn some extra cash after school. True, it could happen that the stock boy who's asked to do the job is a kid who's been tinkering with chain-driven vehicles since his tricycle days and who knows bikes inside out and who is a conscientious and meticulous and dextrous mechanic, etc., etc. It *could* happen, but Jimmy the Greek would give you heavy odds that it won't happen. You don't want to make that kind of gamble with your safety. The practice of having bikes put together by the inept is so dangerous that some states are now considering making it illegal for anyone but a licensed technician to assemble bicycles.

There is a variation on this theme, which might be called the Pandora's box gambit. This is when you buy a bicycle in its box and attempt to assemble it yourself. I strongly advise against lifting the lid for all the above reasons plus a few more. Even that stock boy we've been maligning will probably do a better assembly job than you will, because he at least has *some* experience at it. Maybe after you've had your bike for a while and have done a lot of the repairs and really understand a bicycle, maybe then you could do a halfway decent job of putting a bike together. But right at the beginning, no. (And even later, don't you want a slightly better than halfway decent job?)

Assembly, though, is not the only hitch with a bike in a box. What if, as so often happens, a part is damaged or even missing? How are you going to shake another part out of the vender without hours of frustration and piles of letters to consumer-action reporters? As a matter of fact, without experience with bikes and bike assembly, how are you even going to know if a part *is* damaged or missing?

Another delightful statistic: 85 percent of the people who buy a bike in a box wind up in a bicycle shop getting it put in running order.

PROMISES, PROMISES: A store that specializes in bicycles is able to back up what it sells. Most bike shops urge—even insist—that you bring your bike in after you've ridden it a few weeks to have it checked over. The chain may need tightening, ditto the brake cables. All kinds of little but important adjustments may be necessary, and many of these only appear after a shakedown period. Other venders of bikes seldom offer this post-purchase adjustment service, and if they do, it's rather a hollow gesture, since the only person around to do the adjustment would be someone like that fabled stock boy in his legendary spare time.

Then, too, what happens if your bike should be delivered with an invisible but major defect? All new bikes go snap, crackle and pop for the first several miles, but if yours goes bang, you have more than a minor adjustment problem What store but a bike shop has the tools, the know-how and the replacement part to make it right under the guarantee? The bike shop also has something else that may be even more important. They have the *desire* to make the bike right. Their business is bikes and bikes alone. They know they're going to make it only with satisfied customers giving out the good word of mouth. They care and they care a lot. The hardware store has its lawn mowers and power saws. The drugstore has its aspirin and corn plasters. The department store and the discount house have their everything. If their bike business falls off, it doesn't make all that much difference. They care a lot less.

LET THE BIKE BUYER BEWARE: Before we start canonization proceedings for all bike shop personnel, however, let's admit that no one group can be all good. There are a few flat tires and broken spokes even in this noble breed. Any merchant is in business to make money and will sometimes try to get you to spend more than you want to or try to sell you accessories you don't really need. Bicycle shop owners and salespeople are only human and some will push the product excessively. In my experience, however, most don't do this. Just as bicycling—at least the way most of us do it—is not a high-pressure sport, the selling of bikes and accessories is much less high-pressure than, for example, the selling of ski equipment.

The problem you will run into in a bike shop, then, is not usually one of fending off a hard-sell. The problem is more likely to come when you run up against one of the two sub-species of bike shop worker: the know-nothing or the know-it-all.

A LACK OF KNOWLEDGE IS A DANGEROUS THING: The know-nothing is a guy who's working in a bike shop strictly to pick up a little money. He has no more interest in and feeling for bikes than he would have for rutabagas if he were clerking in a grocery store. Now it would be okay with me if he knew nothing about bikes, if all he did was sell me what I asked for and if he found out I wanted information, shunt me over to someone else. But no, he is the Great Pretender. Ask him a question and invariably he gives you an answer.

I remember once when I was thinking about a new bike (when am I ever *not* thinking about a new bike?) and I wanted to check out some of the new models. I'd done a lot of talking to cyclists and reading about "testing a bike for 'twang' by bouncing it on the floor." Frankly, "twang" was a concept I couldn't quite grasp. I set out methodically asking bike shop personnel about it.

In one shop in Palo Alto, California, I talked to a genuinely knowledgeable guy, a weekend racer and tourer himself. When I put the twang question to him, he was obviously puzzled and said, "Beats me. I've never heard of it. It's probably some dumb idea those bike-book writers are always throwing around. I *do* know that if you bounced the bike, all you'd be testing would be the tightness of the spokes." I felt I could even buy a used bike from that man.

The next shop in my, as it turned out, vain search for twang was a large shop over the Palo Alto border in Los Altos. There a dapper-looking salesperson approached me on panther feet. As I fondled a bicycle, I said casually, "Say, I've been hearing a lot about testing a bike for twang. Could you tell me exactly what twang is?"

"Twang . . ." hmmmmmmmmmmm (fleeting flash of confusion). "Twang . . . oh, yes, *twang*." Smiling triumphantly, he snapped his fingernail against the top tube of a bike, making a hollow sound. "This is twang."

He snapped his fingernail against the top tube of another bike. "You see this one is made of Reynolds tubing. It has a much better twang." (I could tell no difference.)

"You definitely should always test for twang," he

advised.

"Oh, I will, I *will*. Thank you for the advice," I said, moving toward the door.

There you see the difference between a knowledgeable person and a know-nothing. If you ask a knowledgeable person a dumb question, he will admit confusion. He's secure in his knowledge and he doesn't have to fake it. Ask a know-nothing a dumb question and you'll get a super-dumb answer.

DON'T GET SMART: But bad though know-nothings are, I vastly prefer them to know-it-alls. As I mentioned earlier, bicycling is an extremely opinionated activity. Anyone into it for over five minutes starts developing very firm and positive opinions on everything. There's nothing wrong with this as long as opinions are presented as opinions. What I resent are those who try to palm off their personal opinions and prejudices as universal biking truths.

I remember asking one San Francisco Bay Area bike shop owner about how many women preferred a woman's frame and how many preferred a man's.

"I don't care how many women prefer a woman's frame," he said, swelling visibly, "seventy percent of the women who buy a bike in this shop go out with a man's frame whether they came in for one or not."

When I asked a similar question of another bike shop owner in the area, "Do you think a woman should get a woman's or a man's frame?" he answered casually, "It doesn't really matter. Either one's all right. The important thing in biking is to enjoy yourself. I think a person, man or woman, should get the style of frame that he's most comfortable with." If I lived in the Bay Area, I know where I'd buy my bike.

I actually did buy one bike from a know-it-all, although he didn't show his garish colors until I came in for the shakedown period adjustment. The chain was rubbing and scratching. A cycling friend analyzed the problem as a slightly out-of-alignment frame.

When I took the bike back to the shop, the know-it-all ranted to the effect that the frame *couldn't* be out of alignment as he had never in his life sold a bike with a frame that was out of alignment. And, as a matter of fact, the chain *couldn't* be rubbing anything unless I was shifting it wrong. His chains *never* rubbed. Every time I brought the bike in to him because something was wrong, I was always told that nothing *could* be wrong, because he had thirty-five years' experience with bikes, he knew how to put them together, and he could tell at a glance that the bike was perfection itself, as were all the bikes he assembled and sold.

Since I wanted to enjoy myself biking, as the Bay Area shop owner had suggested, I decided to avoid ulcers by avoiding Mr. Perfection. I found another shop where the owner/mechanic, with nary a screech about his prowess, quietly and efficiently corrected the many and varied flaws in this bike, including some stripped threads in the pedals. Correction. He didn't quite fix everything. Even he couldn't completely stop the dragging chain. It still does it in one gear, because, as he noticed immediately, "The frame is slightly out of alignment."

These are extreme cases, of course, and you may never run across anything except the sainted bike shopkeeper type. But always be at the ready. Don't let a know-nothing fill you with false counsel, and don't let a know-it-all push you around. That way you'll wind up with a bike on which you can truly enjoy cycling.

OFFICIAL PRONOUNCEMENT: Some of the difficulties you encounter with bike shop personnel, however, are not so much *their* problem as *your* problem. I am referring to the dilemma of how to pronounce the foreign cycling words—especially the French ones.

My first experience was with the name of the derailleur manufacturer, Huret. I've had a couple of years of French and I knew it should be pronounced something like yur-ray, with a bit of a throat-clear on the *r*. And yet nobody says duh-rye-yur for derailleur—at least I knew that much. It's always Anglicized to dee-railer; so I assumed that when talking to a simple beardful youth in a bike shop in Victorville, California, hardly the cultural center of the West, that all of us straightforward, unpretentious Americans would Anglicize Huret to hugh-ret, with the accent on the first syllable. Not wanting to come off as a phony, that's what I did. The young man quickly made it clear, by archly and pointedly referring to the mechanism as a yuh-ray, that I was a bumpkin and a clod as well as an ignoramesse.

Okay, so the next time I was bike shop prowling in Montrose, California, I noticed they had a good stock of the French bike, the Follis. Fine. Since Montrose is a suburb of Los Angeles and several degrees less bucolic than Victorville, when I asked the attendant something about the bike, I pronounced it like the first word in Folies Bergère. He looked blank and I could see his mental wheels spinning. Finally something clicked and he said, "Oh, you mean the Foll-iss?"

My next problem was with another well-known brand, the Bertin. A friend owned one and I was discussing its merits with him. Should it be, I wondered, the French way, bear-tain (nasally on the end) or should it be Americanized to sound like Elizabeth Taylor's ex-ex-husband. I pondered and fretted. I can't remember what I finally mumbled out. I would have been wrong either way, because in this particular case or with this particular person it was pronounced bert-teen, as if it were Spanish, sort of.

With mixte, that unisex frame design halfway between a man's frame and a woman's frame, I went the French route and called it a meekst. Wrong again. It is always, even in such learned lands as Cambridge, Massachusetts, and Berkeley, California, pronounced mix-tee. Oh, well.

SHOPPING FOR A SHOP: Besides the ideal personnel, what else do you need to look for when shopping for a shop? Propinquity is a great virtue. If the shop is located just a few blocks away, it's a terrific advantage when it comes to getting the shakedown inspection and warranty work done.

When checking out a shop, you might look for a kind of smell of efficiency about the place. This is usually most evident—or missing—in the repair section. Is it clotted and stacked with bikes needing work done? Or is it a deserted village with the mechanic drumming his fingers on the counter or not there at all? Obviously neither of these situations augurs well. Better a shop with a number of bikes finished, a number of bikes waiting to be worked on, and a mechanic briskly engaged in setting a cycle or two to rights.

Another significant plus for the bike shop is if the owner himself rides. I don't mean he has to be a racer or an ex-racer or a 200-mile-a-weekend tourer. I just mean does he enjoy getting on a bike and pedaling around? In other words, does he have as much feeling for bikes and biking as he does for dollars and cents?

It's nice if your nearest local shop is large and vastly stocked with a great number of bikes and accessories, but you shouldn't be put off if it isn't. Contrary to the sports cliché, a good big shop doesn't necessarily beat a good little shop. Some of the outstanding shops in the country like the Cupertino

Bike Shop in California and the Braxton Bike Shop in Missoula, Montana, are small in size but large in quality.

A BRAND IN THE HAND: One problem you may run into is that the shop that you like best may not stock the bike brand you like best. Most shops handle only one or two major manufacturers. It's not always easy or even possible for them to special order other makes of bikes.

My advice to you in this case is to consider switching bike brands to one your chosen shop does stock. In the same price range bikes made by different manufacturers are strikingly similar. As we've already seen, many bike manufacturers make nothing at all. They just put together their particular selection of frames and components purchased from someone else, the same someone elses other manufacturers buy their components from. Let bike aficionados argue forever over the relative merits of a Peugeot or a Gitane or a Fuji or a Bianchi or a Raleigh or a Schwinn, if you strip away the emotion along with the decals, you'll find that price, rather than brand, makes the biggest difference as long as you stick to one of the first-line companies.

An additional advantage to buying a brand your favored bike shop stocks is that they'll be more familiar with its idiosyncrasies and be more likely to have the part to fix it with in stock.

Still, I'd be the first to admit that with certain bikes synergism seems to take place and, at least to you,

the bike is more glorious than the sum of its components. Then by all means, even if you have to drive a
couple of hundred miles to the shop where it's sold,
get it. The magic magnetic bike appeal that one bike
will have for you over another can't be discounted.
You're bound to get more joy and pleasure and action
out of a bike that electrifies your spirit than out of
one with a great deal of the ho-hum factor in its
make-up.

Your local bike shop people will understand if
you're compelled to buy a bike somewhere else.
After all, they're probably bike nuts, too.

FAULT-FINDING: The reason I've ranted so loud and
long about picking out a bike shop is that I believe
that finding a good bike shop with personnel you can
trust is vital. Most of us are never going to know
bicycles well enough to tell a peach from a lemon.
There are endless inspections a person is supposed
to make to check out a bike. You strum the spokes to
discover if they all have the same sound, indicating
the same tension. You sight down the frame and try
to figure out if it's in alignment. You spin the wheels
while peering through the fork and the seat stays
(one at a time, of course) to see if the rims are true
and the wheels turn smoothly and easily. You grab
the wheels and try to move them from side to side to
ascertain if they are loose or not. You turn the wheel
so the valve is at 3 o'clock, then let go and see if the
tire slowly turns on its own delivering the valve to 6
o'clock.

Some experts even go so far as to recommend that you take the chain off the chainwheel and spin the crank to see if it turns smoothly and stops gradually. Others tell you to place your foot on the crank and, grasping the frame by the down tube and the seat tube, bend the frame toward you to see if it feels resilient. And then there's always that good old bouncing the bike around the floor to test it for a firmly attached headset, that infamous twang, and God knows what else.

All of this cyclo-mayhem certainly won't endear you to the bike shop people and may even get *you* bounced. But aside from offending the bike shop personnel, which doesn't make all that much difference, because, after all, you are contemplating spending your money with them, the fact remains that, except for obvious problems like a bulge in the tire or a bolt hanging by a thread, there's very little an amateur can tell about the bike's condition until he's ridden it for a while. A quick spin around the block won't do it. Only after a good number of miles do the flaws, if any, begin to rattle out. Then all of your careful pre-purchase inspection of the bike will be for naught if you haven't taken the time to find yourself an honest, conscientious dealer who will make it all right again.

Bicyclical Nomenclature

As well as a shop you can trust, you need a brand of bike you can trust. There are over a hundred firms in the world that manufacture bicycles, some in such unlikely places as India, Poland, and Brazil. I've heard that China now has a bike boom going, but even if you're a raging exoticist, don't purchase a Chinese bike because everything about them—even the wheel size—is different from the American and European brands.The United States has about a half dozen large and well-established bike firms, including such big names as Schwinn, Huffy, and Columbia. The other leading bike-producing countries of the world are France, Italy, Japan, and Great Britain.

What are some of the good, reliable, well-distributed brands that offer a wide range of bikes and stand behind their product? To start with I'd mention Follis, Fuji, Gitane, Motobecane, Nishiki, Peugeot, Raleigh, and Schwinn. From there on out the list could be almost endless, because many imported bikes are available here only in a limited number of shops and only in limited areas of the country and only in limited price ranges. Just to sprinkle a few good names on you, there are Atala, Azuki, Batavus, Bianchi, Bottecchia, Campania, Falcon, Frejus, Jeunet, Mondia, Murray, Puch, Superia, Windsor, and Zeus.

In choosing a brand name some people let national prejudices interfere. For example, one bike mechanic I know is a card-carrying Francophobe who will hardly put a wrench to a Follis, Gitane, or Peugeot. There's one major problem, though, if you do want to exercise your national prejudices in the bike world:

it's almost impossible to tell which country a brand of bike comes from. A bike has few visible national characteristics and the name attached gives you not a clue. It may, in fact, be a positive red herring.

Ferrare, for example, may sound as Italian as spaghetti, but it's really Japanese. Another ostensible Italian, Campania, is technically an American bike, since it's assembled in Van Nuys, California, but almost all of its everything is made in Japan.

Want to make a guess as to where Windsors are made? If you guessed Mexico, you're right—and you also must be psychic, since its name is as Mexican as Queen Elizabeth's. Mercier bikes are French. This is not at all surprising, but Mercian might raise your eyebrows since it's English.

Chimo, which is the Eskimo word for "Are you friendly?" comes out of the igloos of Hong Kong and is distributed by a Canadian firm. Mondia and Allegro are Swiss despite their Latinate names and the Echo comes not from a factory in the shadow of the Jungfrau but rather is from Korea. (Sigh!) Is Zeus, like its namesake, from Greece? Of course not. It's a Spanish bike.

You might think Volkscycle comes from the land of the car company of a similar name. Naturally, it doesn't. It's from Japan. What *does* come from Germany? Why, the Vainqueur, *natürlich,* and the Victoria.

If you should ever see a Phoenix—unlikely in the extreme—it will be not from Arizona, but from the

People's Republic of China. And another rara avis from behind the bamboo curtain and which, from its name, might have been made in Trafalgar Square or the Piazza San Marco, is the Flying Pigeon.

On the other hand, the Comrade Cycle Works, which you might think would be as red as revolutionary blood, is located well within the British sector—in Staffordshire, to be exact.

Good old American-sounding Smith and Company is a Danish firm, while Miura, which, considering its name, could and *should* be from Japan, is made in exotic Garland, Texas, U.S.A. Frejus is Italian and Stella is French, when all linguistic logic would tell you that it's just the opposite. So it goes.

It gets to the point that you begin to think Fuji should be Polish and Nishiki Peruvian. But believe it or not, they're both Japanese. When it comes to bike names, you can't count on anything.

The Second Time Around

If you have Colnago taste on a trashmo budget, how about going for a used bike? My answer to this is a heavily qualified maybe.

First off, I *know* you're not the kind of person who'd patronize the midnight bike supply—one of those dark alley, pssssst-have-I-got-a-great-bike-for-you weasels. You know full well that without buyers these guys would turn to something less socially damaging like extortion or diamond smuggling. You know you're as guilty as the thief when you buy one, et cetera, et cetera. But even when you know you're not buying from a crook, the used bike may still not be the best investment for you.

It's difficult to find exactly your right frame size in a used bike. The tendency is to figure, well, it's only a few inches off and it's such a good deal . . . Then there you are with a bike that's too big or too small, either of which will ruin your cycling efficiency, comfort, and fun.

You may or may not be getting your money's worth. Either way can be a problem. Because of basic flaws and worn-out parts that are invisible to the untrained eye, you may fall for a real junker. Its manifold diseases will not become evident until you've put a few miles on it. In the case of this kind of bike virtually every penny you've spent on it will be wasted.

Then again, if you pay $150 for a $300 bike, it may be worth exactly what you pay for it, because it may well be a $300 bike that needs $150 worth of repairs and component replacements to bring it up to its original snuff. If this be the case, wouldn't you be better off spending the extra money you're going to have to wind up spending anyway to get the new, fitted-to-you, guaranteed-by-the-shop bike of your dreams in the first place?

Admittedly, there are a few used bike possibilities that are worth looking into. If you haunt the fancy bike shops in your area, you'll sometimes find "hardly used," very classy bikes advertised on cards on the bulletin board or you may find some used bikes being sold on consignment. If you find one that's your frame size and if it's a bike you've always wanted, anyway, then it certainly bears investigation. Sometimes the seller is a college student who's a meticulous bike freak. He just needs money to go back to school or take a trip or maybe even move up into an even more ethereal level of bikedom. Some of the best-looking and best-sounding deals I've seen are bikes offered by bike shop employees who are upgrading or changing to another bike for some unknown reason. Since they paid less for the bike in the first place, they're not losing very much if they sell it for a fourth or a third off. Also, there's a better than average chance that the bike has been maintained well—although there are slobs in every line of business and as shoemakers' children are said to go barefoot, bike shop employees' bikes may miss getting their bearings greased. But in general you can find some tempting bargains this way. For example, I saw an almost pristine Schwinn Paramount shining in chrome skin in a bike shop. It was ever so slightly used by one of the women employees and was being offered for a couple of hundred less than the going new price. The owner just wanted to change. I suspect she wanted to switch to a man's frame. I came within a millimeter of succumbing to this temptation but it was 2 inches beyond my frame size, reason enough to remain strong.

Sometimes if you buy your used bike through a shop—or one of its employees—they will offer you some kind of guarantee. At any rate, it doesn't hurt to ask. If you make the sale contingent on that, they may agree in order to make the sale.

One thing you can do if you're thinking about buying a used bike from a private party is to take it to your trusted bike shop and ask them to check it out for you. There may be a fee for this, but usually all that's necessary is to promise to let the shop correct any faults for you if you buy it.

One thing a bike shop probably can't do for you, though, is tell you if the price of a used bike is right or not. As I heard a Santa Barbara bike shop owner explain it, "Right now it's a seller's market in used bikes. They're pretty much calling the shots. It's impossible to say from day to day what a used bike is 'worth.'" With the modern world of shortages— including shortages of money for new bike buying— it looks as if this trend in used bike prices may continue.

Another possibility for used bike purchase is the police auction. Recovered stolen bikes that have no identification, no license, and no report of their loss on file are often auctioned off. Usually you can get in ahead of time to inspect the bikes and pick out the one you want to bid on. Friends who have done this report they have saved as much as 50 percent.

CHECKS AND BALANCES: Buying a secondhand bike is easier if it isn't your first bike—or your first bike since childhood days. This is because if you have to check out the bike yourself and decide if the price is right and the bike fit (and fits), you will have to have some basis for comparison.

But if you have to make the judgment on your own and it's your first time around, the points you should check are:

1. Does it look bad? Is the paint chewed and battered-looking? (Particularly be wary of wrinkled or ripply paint, which can—and probably does—mean the bike has been in an accident.) Are the rims all scarred up from sloppy tire changing? Is the chain mucked up with dirt-imbedded grease? Does it, in short, look as if nobody cared? If nobody cared on the superficials, he most likely didn't care on the integrals, either.

2. Does it look *too* good? That is to say, does it have a spanking fresh paint job without a nick? That's suspicious. Most people won't go to the trouble to repaint a bike they're going to sell unless they're trying to cover up something like years of abuse and neglect or perhaps an accident.

3. Is the frame in good shape? This is both the most important thing to look for and the hardest thing to tell. It takes the best trained eye in town to know if a frame is straight because it's straight or straight because it's been bent back into shape. And who can tell if the curve of the fork is a little more curved than it was the day it came out of the factory? There is where you're most likely to go wrong, and if someone sells you a bad bike, this is where the bad is most

likely to be.

4. Are the bearings in good shape? This is a close second-most-likely problem area. When you turn the handlebars, wheels, crank, and pedals, do they turn smoothly and quietly or do they grind and catch, indicating dirt and/or damage? If you hear noises and feel scraping, the best you can expect is to have to overhaul them. (And in buying used bikes it's always best to expect the worst.)

5. Does it have the gears you want? A used bike—especially a used fancy bike—is very likely to have gears that are higher than you have in mind. True, it's easy to have the freewheel sprockets changed to make the gears you want, but you then may have to put on a different derailleur with a greater chain capacity to accommodate them. In bikes one expense often leads to another. Incidentally, beware of used track bikes. These are used, as the name suggests, for racing on tracks. They are lightweight and nifty-looking, but look a little closer. No gears. No brakes. It will take a lot of money and work to make a track bike usable for your purposes and even then it probably won't be right for your purposes.

If the bike passes all these tests and if the seller looks clean, brave, and reverent (preferably wearing a clerical collar or an Eagle Scout's uniform), then you have a fifty-fifty chance of getting a good deal.

chapter 4

BIKE SELECTION,
THE DECIDING FACTORS

COST ANALYSIS: They say that most people, when it comes to buying a bike, spend too much money, buying more bike than they actually need. I think the reverse is true. Most people don't spend enough. A bike is a bike is a bike, they think. Their hair tends to rise when they see a $100 price tag, and they think it's outrageous to spend that much for "just a bicycle." In reality, a price tag of thrice that shouldn't make them turn a hair. Especially it shouldn't when you consider many of these same people plunk down $4500 or $5500 for a car that's likely to become junk in three to five years, while a good bicycle, given proper care, can last a lifetime.

55

Now I won't say that some people don't overdo it in bike buying. There are status seekers in every activity. I know one guy who owns two over-$500 bikes—a Bertin and a Masi—and he never rides either of them because, as he says, "My life is too screwed up right now." (He didn't heed my sage counsel that riding his bikes was an excellent way to get unscrewed up.) The only satisfaction he gets from his two bikes, as far as I can see, is telling impressionable people like me, "I have a Bertin and a Masi," and watching their pupils and irises roll up out of sight. But maybe that's worth $1000 to him. Who am I to say?

THE BETTER, THE BETTER: When it comes to deciding how much to spend on a bicycle, many people reason it out in this manner: "I'm an amateur. I don't need a pro bike. I don't intend to be a racer or a long-distance tourer. All I want is to cycle for exercise and fun and maybe do a few errands. Why should I spend a bunch of money on a bike?"

Russell Davis, co-owner of Pickering Cycles in Tucson, can answer that. He believes even such casual riders should go for as much bike as they can possibly afford—a bike of Reynolds 531 or comparable tubing, double-butted frame and all alloy components. To quote him, "A bike such as this is lighter and niftier, and more responsive and easier to take up hills and thus more fun to ride. Probably the easiest way to describe a modern 531 DB all alloy bike is simply to say that it has 'more horsepower' and thus the responsiveness, et cetera. Such bikes are 'racing bikes' only when ridden by racers . . . but they are easier riding bikes when ridden by anyone."

Okay, so Davis is in the business of selling expensive handmade frames, but I'm not and yet I agree with him. When I got my ultimate bicycle, I took my first ride on it in the company of an energetic friend who had always fed me dust on our previous rides together. This time, she was the one with the dry diet. On hills, which I sprinted while she wheezed, she also did an amount of heart eating out.

A fellow I know in his fifties had a similar exhilarating experience. He invested $500 in a Super Mondia. Immediately after signing the check he felt a wave of that emotion realtors call "buyer remorse" sweep over him. "What the hell am I doing spending half a grand on a bike at my age?" he thought. It took only one ride for him to know the answer. As he put it, "That may be the best $500 I ever spent. It bought me back my youth."

By stretching logic only slightly you could, in fact, think of a more expensive bike as an economy measure. The better the bike, the more you'll enjoy riding it and hence the more you will ride it, and eventually the less per mile the cost will be.

What is a "more expensive" bike? To put it in mournful numbers, it can run you around $400 and if you spring for all prime components, upwards to $700. Before you throw down this book and run shrieking from the room, be of good cheer. I have for you what the politicians call viable alternatives to the high cost of best bike buying.

HIGH CAMPY: One economy measure you can take is *not* to buy a bike with Campagnolo components. In case Campagnolo does not ring bells of recognition for you, let me explain. One of the most commonly dropped names in bicycling circles is "Campy." This is short for Campagnolo, the Italian firm famous for its high-quality components and one of the names that kept appearing in Chapter 2 whenever I listed recommended components. On the more expensive bicycles you may see the terms "all Campy" or "total Campy," which means that everything that can be made by Campagnolo is. And that's a lot of everything, including, as it does: bottom bracket, brakes, chainwheel and cranks, clips, derailleurs, fork ends, gear levers, headset, hubs, pedals, seat post, and tools.

That's also a lot of price tag, because Campy prices are high and, like everything else, still climbing almost to the point that you need a shot of oxygen when you pay the bill. Are Campy parts worth it? Again, you have the rule of controversy. Some say, yes, absolutely, nothing can match Campy for perfection in components. Campy fans claim that you can always rely on Campy's precision and quality control.

And then again there are a growing number of mumbles that Campy is overrated and certainly overpriced and not all that reliable, what with today's Italian labor problems. Mainly many believe that what Campy now offers is snob appeal. Bike manufacturer Lloyd Doctor says that Campy's high price is actually one of their marketing gimmicks. They could sell their components for much less, but then they wouldn't sell as many. People *want* to spend a lot for Campy stuff. It's something like Joy perfume, which advertises itself in the *New Yorker* as "the costliest."

The anti-Campy faction maintains you can do as well buying other good alloy components. Shimano Dura-Ace components, for example, are around one third less in price. Shimano is trying hard to catch up with Campy, so hard, in fact, that I've heard a rumor that Campy is suing them for copying some of their designs and that Shimano is returning the litigious favor.

There's only one way to find out how you personally feel about Campy components, and that's to try them. I myself got so tired of Campy braggers that I marched out and bought that all-Campy ultimate bicycle I mentioned previously. This bike weighs only 25 pounds, while my everyday bike weighs 32 pounds. I mounted it, I sailed off—or rather *it* sailed off, because a bike like this seems to propel you instead of your propelling it. Three blocks and I had made up my mind. I adore Campy.

Still, eschewing Campy is a way to save money. It's like getting a Datsun 240Z instead of an Alfa Romeo. You'll still have a great machine.

STAIRWAY TO PARADISE: If you're not certain that biking is going to be such an integral part of your life that you want to invest heavily in it or if you'd love to buy a super whoopee model but just don't happen to have the extra money lying around, then you might enjoy buying a lesser bike and upgrading it a component at a time. This is what I did once with an everyday 10-speed.

Here's the method of attack. First you shop around for a moderately priced bike, say, around $150. You then gradually replace each component with a better one, as you feel a need for increased efficiency and decreased weight. You could, for example, switch from your heavy steel cottered crank to a lightweight alloy cotterless one. This lets you drop around a pound and a half of low-down moving weight, the most significant kind. I think when I added my alloy cotterless crank it made the most dramatic difference of any component.

Then perhaps come alloy rims and hubs and pedals and an upgraded derailleur and shifters and so on until in a year or two or three you will have changed every component to a lighter and better model.

Then comes the giant step for bikekind—the frame. You buy yourself a handmade wonderful in Reynolds 531 or Columbus or some such double-butted tubing. This is the big step in money, too—over $200—but if you've been at biking for a few years and replaced all those other components with better ones, you know you're really into the sport and the money won't be wasted.

Actually you can easily afford a new frame, because as soon as you get it, you'll find you have a bike to sell—your old frame plus all the original components which you've gradually replaced. Now you put them back on their frame and instantly you have an extra bike for sale.

You don't have to sell the original bike. In fact, it's a good idea not to. It makes a dandy spare for when your new wondercycle is having work done on it. It's also handy to have a bike to rob parts from in an emergency on Sunday when all the shops are closed. Besides all that, you might like to have an extra bike with which to do missionary work with your friends. I myself like to use an old bike on trips by plane. When the airlines do their inevitable baggage manhandling, it doesn't destroy my soul quite so much when they wreck a secondary bike.

Not only is upgrading by this method good for those of us who are unable or unwilling to lay out a huge pile of money all at once, but in a way it's more fun. You really appreciate and enjoy each new component as it comes. You can plot and shop for and savor the thought of each new upgrading. "Shall I replace my Huret Allivet gears with a Suntour GT or a Shimano Crane or (delicious shudder of financial horror) a Campy?" "Shall I go for Phil Wood hubs next?"

As Russell Davis says, "We find people who really have to hunt hard to find something on which to spend money once they've bought a complete and final bike. The fun is somehow gone."

There are two minor flaws in this gem of a plan. The first is, it's more expensive to build up your bike a component at a time. In the long run it could cost a hundred or two more than buying the whole shebang. This is partially because import costs for individual components are higher than for whole bikes and partially because it's possible for a bike manufacturer to sell the whole for less than the sum of the parts. Since he buys parts in quantity, he gets a better price on them than an individual does buying them singly and retail at that. And there's the cost of having each component added, if you can't do it yourself. Yet it's still a lot less painful to lay out a modest sum gradually than a larger sum all at once.

The other problem has to do with frames. To quote Davis again, "The only real problem is the French [or Italian] frames. The sizes and threads are all different from anyone else. The best idea is to stay (for example) English. That is, convert a cheaper English bike into a better English bike with no problems, etc." Larry Branson, who performed all the transplant surgery for me with nary a rejection, told me you can easily upgrade with a Japanese or an English bike to start with, since they all have English threading.

If you're really going wild on your frame and having it custom-built to your specifications, you can order it with any threading you want. And well you should be able to, since the frame alone can cost up to $450.

STOP THE MUSIC: Here's another possible saving play in the upgrading game. You may find that after you get all those great components on your old frame you're perfectly happy and don't need to spring for a hand or custom made frame. It could happen. If your old frame is holding together and doing the job for you, you may decide the few pounds you'll shed with the new frame won't make $250-$450 difference in your ride. Bike manufacturer Lloyd Doctor says the quality of the components is a much more significant factor than the quality of the frame. On the subject of frames he says, "Look at it this way. If you ate a big meal that put a few extra pounds into your stomach and then went out for a ride, how much different would your bike's performance be? It's the same with a few extra pounds in the frame."

Here we enter into an area of controversy about as raging and insoluble as Swift's over which end a boiled egg should be eaten from. Some cycle wizards maintain a bike can be no better than the quality of the frame. They consider that it would be folly going on insanity to put good alloy components on anything but a top-grade frame.

Others who are equally knowledgeable agree with Doctor. They think that, except for racers, the importance of the frame is overrated, especially in recent years with all the Reynolds 531 advertising. The choice is yours, as well it should be, since the money spent is yours, too.

CHEAP AT HALF THE PRICE: Now we shift into the lowest financial gear and consider the under-$100 10-speed bike. If you buy one of these, you're going to be getting the worst of everything, including tension headaches and ulcers. Many reputable shops won't even stock a 10-speed at that price. Both shop owners and manufacturers know that a bike of this low quality will spend more time being repaired than being ridden, and no matter what's done to the bike, the customer will never be happy with it.

Here's my one lone flat unhedged nonvacillating statement: Do not buy a new 10-speed that costs under $100.

HAPPY MEDIUM: Between the minimum and the maximum bike purchase there falls the medium. For around $250 you can get what the knowledgeable folk at Sink's Bicycle World in Marion, Indiana, call "a real fine machine . . . the best buy for the money." This kind of bicycle includes such niceties as the best double-butted tubing throughout, an alloy cotterless crank, quick release hubs and, best of all, a total weight of only around 25-27 pounds.

You could be happy on a bike like this for a mighty long time, maybe even forever. Naturally, upgrading is possible here, too, and then when you've completed the process, you wind up with two excellent bikes—a Pike's Peak and an Everest of the bicycle world.

SIZING UP YOUR BIKE: Newspaper ads for discount, department and drugstore bikes are about as entertaining as the comic section. Not only do they tout their caliper brakes and all-steel frames and racing handlebars as if they were something really rare and special, but they often announce with pride and joy that "this is a 27 inch bike." They refer, of course, to the tire size, which is meaningless, since all adult 10-speeds have 27-inch tires. A 27-inch frame size would be appropriate only for someone approaching Wilt Chamberlain in his growth pattern.

Frame size is the important size dimension, not wheel size. Adult frames range from 19 inches to around 25 inches, with fewer available on each end than in the middle. Not all bikes are available in all frame sizes. Far from it. Many of the better quality bikes are available only in 23-inch and 25-inch frames, a form of sizeism that those of us who dwell closer to the ground find infuriating.

I've seen charts that tell you what frame size you should have according to your height. This method is totally unreliable. Frame size is more related to your leg length than to your height. The only truly accurate way to find your frame size is to straddle the bar of the bike with your feet flat on the floor. You should be wearing the shoes you intend to ride in—no platforms or heels. What you want is a bike on which you have ½-inch to 1-inch clearance between your nether regions and the bar.

According to frame-builder Albert Eisentraut, most Americans buy frames too big for them because of our national tendency to want the biggest material possessions we can get our hands—or our seats—on. I would narrow this slightly, if I can without sounding like a female chauvinist sow, and say this is predominantly a male trait. The guy I mentioned before who has the Bertin and the Masi has both of them in a 24-inch frame, when according to his measurements he should be riding a 21-inch. He even admits they're too big and graphically and saltily describes what almost happens to him when he has to make a sudden stop. "But I don't care," he says with a carefree grin, "I like riding a big frame." It's the old John Wayne big-man-tall-in-the-saddle syndrome.

Besides being potentially hazardous to your health and the continuation of the family line, riding a frame that's too large is inefficient and wasteful of energy. A bigger frame takes more material to build and if there's more material, it stands to reason that it's heavier. Why pay extra money for lightweight tubing and all-alloy components and then add gratuitous ounces with a frame that's too large for you?

It's well to ascertain your frame size right off. Then when you're bike shopping and find what may be the bike of your heart, you'll be able to ask if it's available in your frame size. (Sometimes it will have to be ordered for you.) If it isn't available, you can eliminate it before you're hopelessly hooked.

FRAMING FOR YOUR CONSTITUTION: You hear a lot of talk about frame angles. What this boils down to is that the track bikes used by racers have steeper angles (73° or 74° seat-tube and head-tube angles) and are higher and more upright-looking. Touring bikes, which are more comfortable for recreational riders, are more stretched-out-looking (72° angles).

A beware is, don't let a shop sell you a track bike because they happen to have one on hand. One shop owner really put the hard sell on me to buy a Motobecane Team Champion ("Strictly a racing machine, limited production. Made for Motobecane racing team. Exported to the United States whenever possible."). He said it was the only one available in the country with a 19-inch frame. I resisted, knowing that for my kind of riding I needed a little—let's face it—a lot more flexibility to sop up road bumps.

Because of their frame angles, track bikes are rigid. At least, this is partially the reason for their rigidity. Albert Eisentraut says, "The angles, the fork rake, and the chain stay length of any frame are the most important factors in determining a finished bike's stiffness or limberness . . ."

Lloyd Doctor considers the significant stiffness factor in a bike frame to be the seat stays. The thicker they are, the stiffer the bike will be. He also believes you should ride a bike as stiff as you can be comfortable on. The unfortunate part of this admonition is that you probably won't know what you're comfortable on until after you've ridden several bikes over a period of time.

In general, though, I've found stiffness is a very subjective thing, especially with the more advanced bike freaks. If a rider likes his bike and the way it handles and he knows that stiffness is a compliment to make to it, he says he has a nice stiff frame. If he doesn't like the ride, he calls the frame "whippy."

BRAKING POINT: It's my belief that it's not necessary for any of us to sweat the decision between high-quality centerpull and high-quality sidepull brakes. They'll both do the job.

There's a lot of choice, though, on a few less basic feature of brakes. The better ones are usually of the quick release variety. Most commonly these have a little button on the brake lever. When you press this button, it opens up the arms so you can remove the tire without a struggle. Since the tire is wider than the rim, a struggle is what you'll have without this handy button.

Another variation is what are called safety brakes. These are additional brake levers located underneath the crossbar of drop handlebars. I have read and heard rantings that these are the opposite of what their name says. They are *unsafe,* because they don't exert enough force to stop you in an emergency. In my personal experience, however, I find they stop just about as well as the normal levers. When I'm riding with my hands on the crossbar, as I usually am, I can hit them a lot faster than I can those dangling down at the ends of the handlebars. Consequently, they actually stop me a lot *more* quickly. I agree with the man from Hermosa Beach who wrote a letter to the Los Angeles *Times* about bike brakes and said, "The brake hand levers on the butterfly handlebars are suicidal. The rider needs the handspan of King Kong to quickly and easily apply the brakes."

But just to make sure that my lack of disasters with safety levers is not unique, I checked with about ten bike shops to see if they had heard of or done extensive repair jobs on bikes that had been smashed in an accident because of safety lever failure. Their answer was, "Never." Of course, *any* brake, safety or regular, can let you down if it's out of adjustment.

GEARING UP AND DOWN: Your choice of gears will determine whether you zip along and leap hills with relatively little effort or plod along and creep hills— or even walk them—with a great deal of effort. On a 10-speed bike what you have are ten gear choices. Each gear moves the bike forward at a different rate. With high gears each stroke of the pedal sends the bike a high number of inches forward; with low gears each stroke sends the bike forward a low number of inches. Generally speaking, high gears take a high amount of effort; low gears take a low amount of effort.

Gears are confusing because they're expressed in three different ways. One person, when asked what his lowest gear is, will say, "I have a 46 by 28," meaning he has 46 teeth on his smallest chainwheel sprocket and 28 teeth on his largest sprocket on the rear freewheel.

Another may express his low gear in terms of gear ratios. He would get the ratio of his lowest gear by dividing the number of teeth on the smaller chainwheel by the number of teeth on his largest freewheel. The 48 x 28 gear mentioned above would be 1.6.

The third and most common way of describing gears is by gear number (also often called·gear ratio, just to compound the confusion). This number is arrived at by multiplying the gear ratio by 27, which is the diameter of the wheel in inches. The low gear we were referring to in the first two examples would have the gear number of 43.

When you have ten gears, all this dividing and multiplying by 27 sounds like a lot of work and it is. Fortunately, gear charts for this third way of expressing gears are readily available. There's one in Appendix D to help you calculate your own gears. Here's an example of how you do it. On my No. 2 bike I have a freewheel with sprockets of 14, 17, 22, 28, and 34 teeth. These go along the top of the chart. Then I have chainwheels of 52 and 39 teeth. These I put alongside. Then working with the chart in Appendix D I fill in the gear numbers, like this:

	14	17	22	28	34
52	100.3	82.6	63.8	50.1	41.3
39	75.2	61.9	47.9	37.6	31.0

I've also typed these gears on a strip of paper which I've taped to my handlebars so I can refer to them as I ride and know what gear I'm in and figure what gear I want to shift into. Later this becomes automatic, but in the beginning it's very helpful to have the calculations before you.

Just to make a confusing situation still a little more so, I should add that sometimes these gear numbers are called inches, as in the statement, "I have a 36-inch low gear" or "I was pulling an 87-inch gear." This talk about inches gives the impression that it has something to do with the number of inches the bike moves forward. I have, in fact, heard knowledgeable people and authoritative bike books say flat out that gear number means "the number of inches one revolution of the cranks in a specific gear will drive a bicycle." Not so. And what a shame it's not so, because it would be very simple and logical if it were. As it is, it's very illogical, since it's based on history, never an area of life famous for its logic.

Let me muddy the water further with a parallel example. In England in the pre-decimal days they often expressed prices in terms of guineas, although there was no longer a coin by that name in English currency. The English knew this long-lost coin was equal to two pounds two shillings, but mighty confusing it was to an outsider who had nothing to relate it to. History and tradition had left their mark on the English monetary system. And history and tradition have done the same thing with gear numbers in inches.

Gear numbers in inches are based on the old penny-farthing bicycle days when a bicycle had a large front wheel and a small rear wheel. The number refers to the inches the diameter of the front wheel would be, if you were back in the penny-farthing days. The larger the front wheel, the faster the bike would go. A 90-inch wheel, if they could make one that big, would have been a fast mover indeed. Today with our gear system a 90-inch gear is also a fast gear and a 28-inch is low and slow, but much easier to pedal.

If you're curious about the number of inches a crank will drive you forward in different gears, you have to multiply your gear number by that rotten number that never comes out even, pi (3.1416). If you're not a fanatic for precision, you can just multiply the gear number by 3 and get a good approximation of the number of inches you move forward in each gear.

PLAYING THE NUMBERS: Now that we all understand those gear numbers, what numbers should you have on your bike? That depends to a certain extent on your athletic ability and the hills in the area in which you generally cycle. But in my personal opinion, for adult-type cyclists the low gears are the ones I consider important. This is because in any gear combination I've ever seen, you usually have a high gear higher than you'd ever want or need, unless you were the Tour de France leader racing down the incline of Izoard.

As they are categorized, touring gears are generally those that go as low as 35. When you drop down to below 35 you are in the realm of what they call Alpine gears. Below 32 or 30 we get what is scornfully referred to as grannys or super grannys. My counsel is to go at least for Alpine gears, and if you have the guts to bounce off sneers, slip in a granny. The sneers will turn inside out when you're pedaling up a hill while others of your vintage and conditioning are walking and pushing.

With the more expensive bikes you sometimes have trouble getting low enough gears for your practical purposes. This is because bike manufacturers—who are always making false assumptions—assume that if you buy a super bike you're a super rider in super shape and wouldn't touch a gear less than 55. Hah!

This situation is, however, most easily rectified. A good bike shop can slip different sprockets on your freewheel to move you down into the land of easy hill climbing. But as soon as this problem is solved, another may pop up. It involves the derailleur. In order to accommodate the increased chain length necessary for the lower gears, you may have to have the shop replace the derailleur that comes as standard equipment on the bike. The Suntour V, the Shimano Crane GT and the Campagnolo Gran Turismo all can handle grannys clear down to Grandma Moses.

If you do all of this switching at time of purchase, the dealer will do it for a minimal charge. It's a lot easier and cheaper to trade a brand-new component for another brand-new component than it is to switch a used component later for a new one.

The dealer will happily switch sprockets and derailleurs, that is, unless you happen to be shopping in Fanaticland. A hapless friend of mine accidentally found himself in such territory inspecting an Allegro. He noticed the bike had a Campy Nuovo Record derailleur and innocently asked if it would accommodate a lower gear.

"Why would you want a lower gear?" asked the shop attendant, raising his sun-bleached eyebrows.

"Why, to get up hills more easily," replied my friend.

"Listen, buddy," the attendant growled, "if you can't ride this bike the way it is, you have no business buying it."

There is this one truth about a pro bike, though. For the same amount of effort you can usually ride in a gear 10 points higher than you can in a lesser breed of bike. You can and should take that into consideration when you make your sprocket selection.

HOW LOW THE GEAR: How do you know what low gears you're getting when you buy a bike? The easiest way is to ask. A good shop attendant should know the gears or at least be able to figure them out in short order for you. Some new bicycle brochures spell them out on the list of specifications. If you're exploring on your own, you can often find the tooth count stamped on the sprockets of the freewheel and the chainwheel. Or if not, you can count the teeth on the smallest chainwheel sprocket and the largest freewheel sprocket and compute the number using the chart in Appendix D. Watch out for the Shimano freewheel sprockets. The large wheels often have every other tooth eliminated and you have to count the spaces in between. Don't worry about the other people in the shop who may wonder what you're up to down there on your knees muttering to yourself.

A word of caution: Don't get so hung up on your low gears that you sacrifice your middle gears. You'll be doing most of your riding with them and you'll want the most variety there. The best balance in gears is to have two lows (30's and 40's), two highs (80's and 90's) and the rest in the middle.

GETTING A HANDLEBAR ON IT: Probably your bike, especially if it's in the middle- or upper-price category, will be seen on the showroom floor with drop handlebars. They are the in thing now. There are many good reasons for their inness. They give you a lot more positions, as you move your hands from top center to top next to brake levers to the bend and to the end with several position variations in between.

Being able to change hand positions is not only more restful, but the different positions help you perform more effectively in different situations. For ex-

ample, the first position is pleasant when you're pedaling along easily on the flat and want to look around
at the scenery. The third position is good when
you're really sweating up a hill, because your back
and arm muscles can help you with the work and the
bent-way-over position cuts down on wind resistance, too. Also, you have better weight distribution,
since you lean on drop bars more than you do on flat
bars. Most experienced cyclists use drop handlebars,
but not all.

Listen to old friend Russell Davis: "I do not believe that one must have only drop handlebars. My
ride-to-school bike (I teach at the University of Arizona) has high handlebars and everyone teases me
about my old man's bike. On the other hand, it is 'full
race' in every way except the bars . . . and I find the
high bars and grips and under bar brake levers to be
much more comfortable when riding in normal
clothes."

Here you incidentally learned one of the reasons a
number of people, especially those of the masculine
persuasion, can't bring themselves to use flat handlebars: self-image. I also admit to not liking the idea of
looking like a little old lady in biking shorts by using
straight, in every sense of the word, handlebars. Consequently, when I bought a new bike, I got the drop
kind. After an initial period of adjustment I got to liking them pretty well, and they did help me out when
I struggled up a hill. But I began to notice that about
95 percent of the time I rode with my hands on the

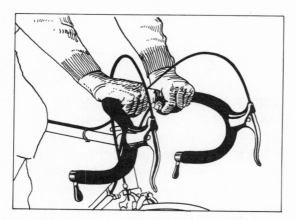

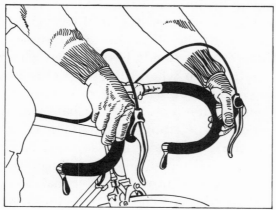

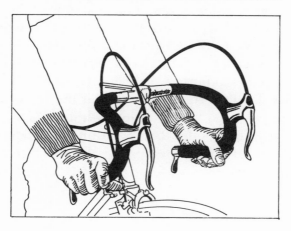

top-of-the-bar position, the better to look around and see the sights. Sightseeing is, to me, one of the prime joys of biking.

Then it happened that my new bike was in the shop getting an upgraded component attached. I was using an old 15-speed I had treated shabbily in my earlier cycling days and had refurbished for penance and practice. This bike has touring handlebars rather than drop style. I found that, Thomas Wolfe to the contrary, you *can* go home again. I was mightily glad to be back with the more upright position. I also found that with my hands farther apart I had much greater control than when they were closer together on the top of the drop bars.

My favorable impression of flat bars was recently strengthened by a study of handlebar safety conducted by the industrial engineering department of the University of Oklahoma. Results of the study showed that flat bars provide better maneuverability and greater visibility. The latter factor permits the rider to react faster in emergencies, too.

I've started leaning even more in the direction of flat bars since I read a warning, "Bicyclists Beware," in the *Journal of the American Medical Association*. Three doctors reported on patients who had developed weak hands (technically ulnar neuropathy) as a result of prolonged bike riding with drop handlebars. "With handlebars in that position, the rider puts strong pressure on the hands, wrists, and forearms as the legs thrust downward on the pedals." All the patients had to give up cycling for several months in order to recoup their hand strength.

From my experience of returning to flat bars I evolved my 20-mile rule. My rule is that if most of your biking is for a distance of 20 miles or longer, the drop handlebars are the best bet. You're going to be in there cranking along, dressed in cycling togs, making tracks, heaving your back into the job, and the drop style bars will conserve energy. If, on the other hand, the over-20-mile excursion is a rarity for you, you might well prefer the flat bars. You should by all means use whatever is most comfortable and enjoyable for you. Forget about your image, if you can. (I myself have a heckuva time doing that.)

If you do opt for the goat horns (as their detractors like to call them) and you have small hands, try to get the randonneur style bars rather than the Maes. Alas, most bikes, except a few French ones, come with the Maes bars as standard equipment. For a few coins your dealer will usually make a substitution for you.

Also, most dealers are delighted to substitute touring bars for drop, because what with the current taste for the drop style, they can always use another set. Personally, I prefer the flatter, straighter style of touring handlebar to the curved-in ones. The former gives what I consider a more comfortable hand position, as the grip cuts across the median nerve instead of paralleling it. (This helps avoid numb fingers.) The one drawback with flat bars is that there's not much selection in quality, as there is with racing bars. It's next to impossible to find alloy touring bars.

The nice thing about handlebars is that you're not married to any one kind for life. If you get one style and don't like it or your riding habits change over the years, it's relatively inexpensive to switch. (You do have to change brake levers, too, though.) But whatever style handlebars you choose, give them a fair trial. The drop handlebars, especially, take quite a bit of getting used to. If you think they're what you'll ultimately be happiest with, try them out for a couple of months of steady riding before you decide you can't cope.

And a final admonition. Avoid at all cost the teenage aberration of taking drop handlebars and turning them around backwards so the ends face forward or up in the air. Not only is this unsafe, but it is weird and there's nothing worse for an adult's self-image than copying teen-agers' weird fads.

DEEP-SEATED PROBLEMS: Generally speaking, if you've decided on your style of handlebars, your seat logically follows behind. The racing saddle is most compatible with the drop bars and the mattress saddle with the touring bars. This is because of the difference in the body's position when you ride with the different bars.

With the drop bars the rider's weight is fairly evenly distributed between his hands and his seat. He leans on the saddle as much as he sits on it. Consequently, the discomfort of that narrow hardness is not all that great. Still, these seats are admittedly *very* hard. A wag once said that they're great for racing, because "the principle behind their design is that the rider goes to beat hell the sooner to get off it." That's not quite true, of course. Racing saddles are really made as hard as they are so as not to dissipate any of the force of pedaling and as narrow as they are so as not to interfere with the pumping of the legs.

Even among racing saddles there are a number of differences. Some are a little wider and don't give you that I'm-impaled-on-a-stake sensation. The narrowest are only 6 inches or 6¼ inches wide. Contrast this with 7½ inches or 8 inches for a mattress type. A moderate width for a racing saddle is 6¾ inches or 7 inches. Most riders prefer leather saddles, because they eventually (and eventually can be quite a spell, usually around 500 miles) conform to your posterior contours with a little help from neat's-foot oil applied to the underneath. (This treatment also means oil-stained pants at first.)

Another method for taking care of the lack of comfort of the leather racing saddle is offered by a Mr. G. G. McGeorge in a letter to *Bicycling Magazine.* "I'm sixty-five and love good, hard cycling. After five years of physical misery associated with trying to soften up a so-called professional leather saddle that came with my Paramount, I finally found a solution to my problem. Build a hot fire outside; throw the saddle on it; stand back, and with a grin watch the damned thing go away."

As far as reputation goes, Brooks is the Campy of leather saddles. Another good brand is Idéale.

Although plastic saddles are nonconformists, some are already contoured and if you find one that

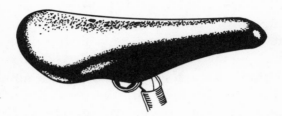

Racing saddle

Mattress saddle

matches your seatprint, it's possible to get instant comfort or at least instant nonagony. Leading brands are Unica, Idéale, and Mesinger. On my best bike I have a very happy compromise. It's a leather-covered plastic saddle, the Unicanitor Brevettata. I like it, because although it's a racing saddle, it's a bit wider and has a bit more give than most. A newly designed plastic seat with contoured comfort pads has the no nonsense name, The Seat. It sells for a hefty $30, is made by Cool Gear.

Mattress saddles, which really would be more logically called spring saddles, are more comfortable and practical when you have the majority of your weight on your seat, as you do when you ride in the more upright position with flat handlebars. The springs of the saddle take up the road bumps instead of your spine. There is a wide range of mattress saddles, more so than of racing saddles. They range from squishy quilted numbers with big round springs in the back to the rather spartan Brooks B72, which has only four looped wires for a spring and is nearly as hard as a racing saddle, although wider. Actually, the Brooks B72 is sometimes not even referred to as a mattress saddle, but rather as a touring saddle. It's an excellent halfway point between the ascetic racing saddle and the decadent mattress. It can be used quite successfully with either drop or touring handlebars. I find its one flaw is that the rivets stick up a little too high around the back of the saddle and tend to poke you.

Be wary of too mushy, too springy saddles. These appear to be as comfortable as carpet slippers. But just as it's not a good idea to walk to the store in your carpet slippers, these super mushies over the long run—in fact, even over the short run—can tire you, chafe you, and generally make you uncomfortable. Not only that, but the more they squish, the more they weigh and, remember, for cycling ease you want to make your bike as light as possible.

In general, the old 20-mile rule holds for racing vs. mattress saddles, just as it did for drop vs. flat handlebars. But since this is Liberty Hall, if you prefer to mix drop handlebars with a mattress saddle or flat bars with a racing saddle, nobody can tell you you're wrong, although I guarantee they'll try.

PEDAL EXTREMITY: When it comes to pedals, there's only one way to go—alloy. Here again we have that low-down moving weight that is so significant and noticeable. For a long while I clung to a set of steel pedals because they were a foldable variety that made it easy to pack bikes in the back of a station wagon without the risk of putting one bike's pedal through another bike's spokes.

Each time in my upgrading program when I added a new alloy component, Larry Branson would shake his head over those steel pedals. For so little cost (if I didn't buy $60 Campys) I could make so much weight difference. Finally, I succumbed. Larry was right. Still, when I pack my bike, I have a nostalgic twinge over the lost folders. I dream of the day when an alert manufacturer makes folders in alloy.

Incidentally, if you think the folding feature would be of more value to you than the weight differential, the only place I know to get the folders is from Ted Van der Kolk, Flying Dutchman Bicycles, 509 E. Broadway, Glendale, California. They were at this writing in the $5 range, but with prices flipping around as they do, it's best to write for an exact quote.

CLIP JOINT: Another good 20-mile-rule candidate is the toe clip. With toe clips the toe of your shoe fits into a clip and you strap your feet in. For a long ride in the wide-open spaces you get a fast 40 percent more power if you're fastened into toe clips and straps. This is because you're pulling when your foot comes up as well as pushing when it goes down. Toe clips also keep your feet in the correct position on the pedals at all times. Toe clips make you look like a genuine hotshot cyclist. Some experts even claim that toe clips are a safety feature! (! mine), as they keep your feet from slipping off the pedals at crucial moments. All cycling experts agree that toe clips are the only efficient, intelligent way to go. I hate toe clips.

Here's my dismal personal experience with clips. When I bought my first 10-speed bike about ten years ago it came equipped with toe clips and straps. I mounted with a certain amount of precarious struggle, got my feet in the clips, bent over to tug the straps, and pedaled off into the traffic of Los Angeles' Pico Boulevard toward my car. Suddenly a stop was required, as it so often is in traffic. Toes remained snugly in clips and there was a mighty splat that resulted in an injured knee that still gives me twinges. Good-bye, toe clips.

Probably the greatest toe clip fanatic in the world wouldn't try to use them in Pico Boulevard traffic or at least he'd keep the straps so loose he could get his feet out instantly (and thereby blow 50 percent of the 40 percent increased power). Or maybe in traffic he'd flip the pedal over so he could ride with the toe clips on the bottom, as I've seen a number of cyclists do in the same way that some of the kids turn their drop handlebars around so they stick up instead of down.

If you do decide to go for toe clips, be sure you get the right size; there are three sizes. Check them out in your bike shop with the shoes you intend to use for riding.

One saving feature of toe clips is that they can be put on and removed and put on again almost instantaneously. Far easier, for example, than changing handlebar styles. So you can have it both ways: toe clips for country lanes and pedal alone for traffic situations.

I've seen some mini toe clips that you use without straps. I feel that these combine the worst of two worlds. They are too small and loose to measurably improve your pedal power and yet they're something of a hassle to get into and out of. They do, however, keep your foot in the right position.

TIRESOME THOUGHTS: As I mentioned in Chapter 2, there are two kinds of bike tires—clinchers and sew-ups. Clinchers are also sometimes called wired-on and unfortunately also tube type. I say unfortunately, because sew-ups are often referred to as tubulars and (now tears begin to form) they are also sometimes called tubeless. Tubeless makes some sense, because the tubes are sewn up inside the tire so that the tire looks as if it's a one-piece item. Since bouncing back and forth from calling bike tires tube type to tubular to tubeless is bound to mix us all up, we'll stick with the old reliable differentiating names of clincher and sew-up.

IT'S A CLINCH: The clincher is the common man of bicycling tires. All but the finest racing and touring cycles are clincherized. A clincher has a separate tube. This is inserted inside the tire. The open edges of the tire have a wire or "bead" running just inside the edge. These beads fit into the rim and hold the tire in place.

SEW JOB: Sew-ups have no imbedded wires. The tube is literally sewn up inside the tire casing. Under the stitching next to the tube there is a chafing tape to keep the stitches from rubbing the tube, which is quite delicate, as tubes go. On the outside of the stitching there is base tape glued on. The tire is in turn glued into the rim along the base tape.

Racers and advanced cycling freaks all use sew-ups. What's so good about them? Light weight, for one thing. Sew-ups and their rims weigh about half as much as clinchers and their rims. They are also narrower. With less low-down moving weight (about

2 pounds less) and less surface contact with the road, sew-ups make riding much faster and easier and give a more fluid-flowing feeling. You almost feel as if you're floating on them. A cyclist friend of mine conducted an experiment with a buddy of his who is about the same size and weight. They rode identical bikes, one with clinchers and one with sew-ups. When they coasted down a hill, the one riding the sew-ups came out a block and a half ahead.

If sew-ups are so heavenly, then why doesn't everybody ride them? Mainly it's because everybody has better sense. They don't want to squander their lives and fortunes and sanity on tire care. Sew-ups are as delicate as Camille in her last stages and they are extremely vulnerable to rocks and thorns and bits of glass and metal. In other words, they're extremely vulnerable to everything that's likely to be all over city streets and country roads.

The sew-up rider has to keep an eye or two on the road surface at all times. He also has to keep a gloved hand continually brushing potentially puncturing debris off the tire surface or he has to have a little "tire saver" attached to the top of the fork to scrape junk off the tire as it rolls through.

The prudent sew-up rider (is that a contradiction in terms?) also at all times carries a couple of complete tires with tubes sewn up inside, because repairing a damaged sew-up is not the kind of activity you do out on the road. It is, rather, the kind of activity you save up for a snowbound winter evening. No, better make that a whole snowbound winter. If you want to see what a grotesque job repairing a sew-up is, read about it in some *Compleat Book of Bicycle Repair for Fanatics*. You won't read descriptions of such aberrant behavior in this book. This is a clean book for normal people.

To top it all off, sew-ups are an economic disaster. They pop as continually as the popcorn machine in the lobby of a hit movie and have about one-twentieth the life expectancy of clinchers. They cost at least three times as much as clinchers, around $15 a copy for cheapies and up to $30 for the best.

Unfortunately, when you shop for a bike, if you're going for a more expensive model, you're almost certain to find it equipped with sew-ups. It's easy to tell this, because the bike will be displayed without any tires on it. Sew-ups are not put on until the bike is sold (another indication of their delicacy). The shop will probably switch rims and tires for you. Don't let any negative mutterings on the salesman's part deter you. And don't, by any means, let him talk you into riding with sew-ups for a while to see how you like them. You'd probably adore the way they ride and, having ridden them, never be happy again with clinchers. Just as it might wreck your marriage if you should go out with Robert Redford or Ali McGraw, it might louse up your on-going relationship with clinchers if you once rode with sew-ups. Since sew-ups are too temperamental for most of us to live with, it's best never to taste their forbidden delights.

THE CLINCHER COMPROMISE: For those of us who are rational enough to realize we want the convenience and durability of clinchers yet still would like to get a whiff of the advantages of the lightness and less road friction of sew-ups, there is a new clincher which is the same size as a sew-up (1⅛ inches instead of 1¼ inches wide). This clincher weighs only a few ounces more than the heavier brands of sew-ups. Right now Raleigh distributes a couple of varieties of these, as do other bike tire manufacturers, such as D'Alessandro, Milremo and Schwinn.

You can use your regular clincher rims with the new narrower clinchers. An additional advantage is that it is easier to remove wheels from your bike with the narrow clinchers; you don't even need quick release brakes.

chapter **5**

FOR WOMEN ONLY

SEXISM AND THE
10-SPEED BIKE

Well, my dear sisteren, it's easy to find out what
the bicycle establishment thinks of us. Just look inside the pages of their publications, especially those
aimed at the trade. There you'll see the likes of an ad
featuring a bunnyesque blonde wearing hot pants
and clog shoes and straddling a bike. The subtle caption reads, "Made in Sweden." Other bike models—
female human variety—are found wearing sandals,
knee-high leather boots or, best of all, they're barefoot. There's nothing more comfy than biking barefoot with rattrap pedals or toe clips!

Even the respected aficionado publication, *Bike World,* illustrated an excellent article by Dr. Creig Hoyt on "Women in Cycling" with a margin-to-margin navel extravaganza of bikini-clad nubile maids, again (sigh!) barefoot. My special favorite, though, is a full-page ad which appeared regularly in *Bike World* for Mercier brand bicycles. The caption reads, "I just bought my son his first bicycle," and the illustration shows the proud father with his tiny (male) baby perched atop the seat of an adult-size bike the father intends to use until his son is old enough for it. The motto of the firm is, "Mercier, for yourself and your son . . . it lasts that long." In this ad the wife stands beaming proudly behind the bike. Presumably she'll be at home pickling peaches while old dad is out wheeling and dealing.

Then there's the League of American Wheelmen. They've been hassling over a name change. Their bulletin is loaded with impassioned letters pro and con. And why do most of those who want a name change want it? Not, mind you, to make the name more sexually inclusive, something like League of American Cyclists. No, they're only concerned that the initials not spell out LAW, as they now do, because when members wear the organization's emblem on their jackets, they don't want people to be put off by thinking the Wheelmen are members of some kind of parapolice force.

WE ARE FRAMED: The above are all just the surface warts on the hog of bicycle sexism. The real problem lies with bicycle design and manufacture. This is what makes bicycle selection for women such a dilemma. In the end the decision always results in a compromise or, as they say in horse racing, picking the best of a poor field.

Right now the vogue, especially for younger women, is to buy a man's frame, referred to by most men in the trade as the "normal" frame. This sometimes right decision is often made for the wrong reasons—the desire to out-macho the men or peer pressure or simply following the latest fad.

One girl I know, when her own triangle frame bike was undergoing minor repair, refused her mother's offer of the use of her woman's frame model for the ride to school. The daughter said, "I'd rather walk than ride that thing." I've heard the somewhat stronger "I'd die before I'd ride a woman's bike."

Now don't get the wrong idea. There are some very valid reasons for buying a man's frame. Some of those reasons may just apply to you. If you are especially tall and/or especially long-legged, you may be able to get a large enough frame only by buying a man's bike. Most bicycle manufacturers offer only one or two frame sizes in a woman's model (usually 21 inches or 19 inches and 21 inches).

Another situation in which you're automatically sentenced to a man's frame is if you plan to race. There ain't no such animal as a track bike with a woman's frame, and for road racing you'd need the super stiffness of a man's frame.

There are still more examples of male frame supremacy. You can get a far, far greater selection of models in men's frames. In fact, the top-of-the-line bikes of most manufacturers come only in men's frames, and unfortunately for smaller women, often only in frame sizes of 21 inches and over. Couple this with the fact that bike shops tend to stock many more men's frames than women's and you can see the masculine advantage.

Resale value is also a bit better for men's bikes, since they're in much greater demand. (For the same reason they are better rip-off candidates.) Two other minor men's frames pluses: they fit better on a bike carrier, and if they get bent out of shape in an accident, they're easier to bend back into shape.

Now if you're the type who wouldn't be caught dead on a woman's frame, it may distress you to learn that a man's frame, for all its advantages, may pose some serious problems for you. The underlying drawback is that the bike manufacturers assume that men's bikes are going to be ridden by men, and they build them accordingly. As you may have noticed, men and women are physically different. I do not here refer to primary or secondary sex characteristics, but to what might be called tertiary sex characteristics—that is to say, bone and muscle structure. Men have wider shoulders and longer arms than women; proportionally they have more muscle and less fat than women.

Often the seat of a man's bike is placed too far back for a woman, and it can't be adjusted far enough forward for comfort and efficiency. This may result in a woman leaning too heavily on her hands, which are less muscle-padded than a man's. On long rides over rough roads this can cause painful nerve damage.

Often the handlebars on men's bikes have too much drop, and it's awkward for us to grab those brake levers with our smaller-sized hands.

Another disadvantage of the man's frame is, as P. T. Barnum would have put it, one of ingress and egress. One bike shop owner summed it up with, "There is no graceful way to get on or off a man's bike." Now grace has never been one of my bags, but ease and safety are, and the woman's frame has both of these, when it comes to mounting and dismounting and stopping and starting. I especially shudder at the thought of a sudden stop when my foot twists or my ankle collapses and I find myself slamming into that wonderfully rigid crossbar with my somewhat less rigid pelvis.

SKIRTING THE ISSUE: They say that the woman's bike frame is designed more for our attire than for our anatomy. Originally the dip in the frame was put there to accommodate skirts. But most of us don't wear skirts all that often any more, especially when engaged in active sports. It is true, though, that if we really make biking a part of our daily lives, then we are going to want to bike in skirts sometimes. A woman's frame is better for this.

As for the woman's frame design being inherently

weaker than the man's, what does it matter? What do you expect to be doing on a bike that's going to break it down? I personally have never seen a woman's bike collapse under normal use. When I pointed all this out to a fellow in a bike shop who was lecturing me on the greater strength of a man's frame, he had no rejoinder. And he was clearly the kind of know-it-all who would have rejoined, if he'd had a rejoinder to rejoin with.

The very small/or short-legged woman who can't straddle a 19-inch man's frame with a little space to spare is *very* well advised to stay off a man's frame for basic safety's sake.

There are not many manufacturers who deign to make a really topnotch bike in a woman's model. The few who will let you into the rarefied atmosphere of the over-$500 bike are Atala (Italian), Mondia (Swiss), and Schwinn (U.S.). It's sad that there aren't more, because when you buy your ultimate bike you like to think of it as being a purchase to last you the rest of your life. Imagine yourself creaking along on your bike at age ninety. What kind of frame would you feel safest and most comfortable on then?

MIXTE EMOTIONS: A compromise woman-style frame is the mixte. The mixte is also known as the unisex frame. The crossbars of the mixte (there are two parallel thin tubes instead of one thick one) are about halfway between the straight-across-the-top of the man's frame and the deep V of the woman's. The bars run straight through to the back wheel, giving three points of attachment there rather than the two of the men's and standard women's frames. This makes it the strongest of the open-frame styles. Personally I

Mixte frame

favor the mixte over all other frame types simply because it's the most elegant-looking thing around.

In Europe where men are more concerned with protecting the actuality of their sexuality than the image of it, many of them ride a mixte for ease and safety. Many of them also ride a mixte for thrift reasons. They're a one-bike family and the woman, who also uses the bike, wants one that can accommodate skirts.

Mixte frames, however, are generally not available in sizes over 21 inches, so, effective compromise though they may be, they can't be used by everyone, Incidentally, when fitting yourself either to a woman's or a mixte frame, straddle a few men's frames, ascertain your size on them and then get that size in the woman's or mixte.

There you have all the frame possibilities except one, which, because of the cost involved, might be called the "Rockefeller Variation." We're talking about a custom-made frame. With one of these you measure your leg length, torso length, arm length, and send these measurements along with your shoe size, height and weight. Then for a mere $250–$450 for the frame alone you can get a bike that fits you to perfection. If you want to order a frame, talk to your bike shop or contact one of the mail-order sources in Appendix C. Keep in mind, though, that not only is the frame itself more expensive this way, but adding the components individually is much more costly than buying an assembled bike.

PENNY WISE, POUND FOOLISH: Now that we've dealt with the parts, let's consider the whole. My most sincere advice to you is to buy the best bike you can possibly afford. And this advice, strangely enough, brings us to another sex problem. Generally men are willing to spend more on sports equipment than women are. It's probably part of the lifelong conditioning that has made every man harbor the suspicion that he's a potential champion and should equip himself accordingly and made every woman believe that she's just playing around and doesn't need any more than the minimal. I've noticed this phenomenon particularly with married couples. You see the "athletic" man clicking along on a $500 all-alloy component pro bike weighing 24 pounds, while his "frail" wife hauls around a 40-pounder costing less than $100. (All the while the man is muttering about how his wife "can't keep up.") With bikes less is more: less weight is more expensive. So the more you spend, the easier your riding will be. When you shop, be sure to do a lot of lifting!

I think this lifting factor has been underrated by women. Women who invest in a really light bike— say, under 25 pounds—have put themselves in an equal-to-men enjoyment and freedom category. When I used to load my 32-pound bike into the station wagon, hang it on the rack, flip it upside-down for tire-changing, or shift it around for locking to a pole, I'd struggle and groan and question how long I was going to be willing to cope with these aspects of the sport. Now when I toss my 25-pound pro bike around, I never have even a fleeting doubt about my till-death-us-do-part love affair with biking.

THE TURN OF THE SHREW: To my mind true liberation consists not of clenching your fist and demanding rights, but of freeing yourself from stereotyping. One of the strongest stereotypes we're locked into is that women are "not mechanical." Balderdash! We would be just as mechanical as the next fellow if we'd been given Erector sets for Christmas instead of sewing sets and if we'd been encouraged to take the wheels off our tricycles to see how they work rather than to stir up mud pies for dolly's tea party.

What we need to do now is de-brainwash ourselves. All things are in our realm, including bicycle adjustment, maintenance and repair. If you can follow a recipe, you can follow bike repair directions. (As a matter of fact, you can follow bike repair directions, even if you can't follow a recipe.) If you have enough manual dexterity to sew on a button, you have enough to handle the basics in bicycle maintenance.

It's my firm contention that women are at absolutely no disadvantage—except psychologically—when it comes to working on bikes. In doing car repair or plumbing some of us just may not have the physical strength to handle the job. But with bikes strength is not a problem. In fact, too much of it is a positive disadvantage. A light touch is vital in working on bikes. Ham-handed brute force strips threads and snaps alloy parts.

It may not be easy for you to get started on bike adjustment and maintenance. For one thing you may have an aversion to getting your hands greasy. Tip from the good old sexist kitchen: to make cleanup easy, spray your hands with Pam before starting to work and scrape your nails over a cake of soap so the grease won't get under them. If you take these precautions and also invest in a can of mechanic's hand cream (available in any automotive store), you can easily clean up from your bike maintenance endeavors and look as if you've been doing nothing grubbier than embroidering rosebuds on pillow cases.

Your other problem may be one of lack of experience. How many women know what a crescent wrench looks like, let alone how to use it? This we'll now rectify with an instant guide to the basic tools of bike repair.

Bikes are put together with:

Screws. Normal, Phillips head.
Bolts.
Nuts (thread onto screws and bolts). Keep in mind that normally you turn a nut clockwise to tighten it and counterclockwise to loosen it.

The basic tools are:

Screwdrivers, for turning screws. The blade end fits into the slot on top of the screw and must be the right size for the slot.
Wrenches, for turning nuts. The kind we'll use is a 6-inch crescent wrench, a very light easy-to-hold tool that adjusts to the size of the nut.
Pliers, for gripping. You use them for twisting or pulling or just holding.

In order to give yourself a philosophy and methodology for working with things mechanical, I recommend reading Robert M. Pirsig's *Zen and the Art of Motorcycle Maintenance*. Reading the whole book would be good for your soul, but if you just want to use it for the practical purpose of handling your bike repairs, read Chapters 24, 25, and 26 to give you the "gumption" (Pirsig's word) to do them. To quote one of his lines, "the real cycle you're working on is a cycle called yourself." You may be amazed to find out how putting a bike together helps you put your own head together.

BODY ENGLISH: What kind of biking destiny can a woman expect from her anatomy? The portents are good. Our human machines can generate just as much energy for cycling as can the human machine of the opposite sex. In fact, in the long haul a woman can outperform a man. Beryl Burton of England often beats all the men in 25-mile time trials. And in most events 25–100 miles in length, thirty-seven-year-old Mrs. Burton, who holds fourteen different world championship medals in women's bicycle racing, wins over men.

Because the female pelvic girdle is placed and shaped differently from the male's and because the chest cavity is lighter and the thigh bones heavier in relation to muscle mass, women have a lower center of gravity. This makes balancing easier, an advantage in a sport like cycling. The female knee joint is also more stable and this further enhances good balance.

One big physiological negative for the female is her body's inability to cool itself as well as a man's. Women have more fat tissue than men and perspire less. The caution here, then, is to be particularly careful not to overexert in hot weather riding.

The medical problems of women cyclists have been reported by only one doctor, the aforementioned Creig Hoyt, medical editor of *Bike World* and self-proclaimed reformed M.C.P. Dr. Hoyt has pointed out that women are more likely than men to suffer painful nerve compression of the hands. The solution to this is to buy yourself a pair of well-padded leather cycling gloves.

Also, Dr. Hoyt has found women cyclists to be especially prone to inflammation of the tendon around the elbow (tendonitis). You can avoid this problem by making sure your bicycle's stem length and handlebar drop are correctly measured and by not allowing your arm to rotate out and up while cycling. This means keeping your elbows in as close to the body as possible.

chapter 6

THE SCIENCE AND
ART OF RIDING

Adjustments

So you've bought your bike. Now what? Do you finally get to hop aboard and ride? Not quite. Not yet. You still have to make a couple of adjustments: the seat and the handlebars.

If you've hit it lucky, the shop has measured you and carefully raised or lowered the seat and nudged it backward or forward and correspondingly adjusted the handlebars. If you've hit the way most of us hit it, none of the adjustments has been made. But that's okay. The adjustments are easy and when you do them yourself you begin to feel you're in charge and that the bike truly belongs to you.

104

How high the seat? The seat should be higher than you think it should be. At least, this is so if you think you should be able to sit on the saddle and have your feet solidly planted on the ground. This does give you wonderful feelings of security, but it is definitely not the most efficient and least tiring saddle height.

Years of cycling research and experimentation and, of course, bickering, have finally yielded the information that when you sit on the saddle with the ball of your foot on the pedal when it's at the point farthest from your seat, you should have a *slight* bend in your knee. Now since getting your saddle at exactly this height involves a lot of trial and error and trial again, there has evolved a scientific formula—the rule of 109 percent. The way it works is you take off your shoes and measure your leg from the crotch to the floor and multiply this by 109 percent. This should be your correct saddle height. You measure the bike from the top of the saddle to the pedal when the pedal again is down and out and farthest from the saddle, and adjust to the figure you came up with.

I felt this formula was too easy and, therefore, not to be trusted; so I approached the seat positioning from the trial-and-error method. I worked over it for about an hour until I got the seat in the just right position as far as leg extension is concerned. *Then* I measured the distance on the inside of my leg and the distance from saddle to pedal and, lo, 109 percent it was. I recommend using the magic formula. It's a great time saver.

Now for two warnings, one mild and one strong. First the mild. Be not distressed if your seat height doesn't feel right at first. It's probably different from the vague and imprecise and ever-changing (with growth) heights you rode as a child. (Note: Almost everybody, if allowed to adjust his seat by instinct— the seat of his pants, if you will—is most likely to have it too low.) But ride for 100 miles with the seat at the recommended height. If it still feels wrong, then make minute adjustments until you're happy and comfortable. Happiness and comfort in biking are, in my opinion, more important than formulae.

Now for the severe warning. You must always have at least two inches of your seat post inserted into the seat tube. Only with this much to spare can you be sure the whole business won't play pop-goes-the-seat-post at some crucial moment. Therefore, it's a good idea to mark the post at the two inch from the bottom point. Requiring the post to be marked this way is one of the possible proposals for the new federal safety regulations, but until something like that's adopted, we have to scratch or paint our own protection.

Okay, now you've taken a wrench and loosened the nut at the top of the seat tube, adjusted your seat to the correct height, and tightened the nut. (If you didn't find a nut there, but a hexagonal hole, you have an expensive seat post and need a special Allen wrench.) Tighten it until it's really tight, but don't apply every ounce of your brute force or you'll strip the threads. This is true in all of bicycle adjustment work. Even I, whose strength is not up there with Sampson, have been known to overpower a bike bolt.

There is still more to the seat adjustment process. Just under the saddle there is another nut on the seat clip. By loosening this you can scoot the saddle backward (farther from the handlebars) or forward (closer to the handlebars) and you can also tilt the seat so that it's higher or lower in the front or back.

How close should the saddle be to the handlebars? The official dictum is if you put your elbow against the nose of the saddle you should be able to touch your fingertips to the back edge of the handlebars. *But.* (Have you noticed there are more buts in bicycling than spokes on both wheels?) *But,* if you move the saddle forward to narrow the gap, you have to make sure you're not moving it too far forward. The front tip of the saddle should range from 1 to 3 inches behind the center of the crank hanger. If you want to be totally accurate on this, you can drop a plumb line from the saddle nose and see where it hits, *but* (here we go again) I don't think it's necessary to be all that fussy.

TILT: While you have the saddle loose, you also have to adjust the tilt so that it is level, up at the nose, or down at the nose. The tilt of the saddle, in my opinion, is strictly a matter of taste and comfort. I had always read and heard from the "experts" that a saddle should tilt up slightly in front. I dutifully tried this, but since I was riding with drop handlebars, when I bent over and pushed hard, I kept almost sliding off the back of the saddle. I put up with this for about a month. Finally, I said the heck with this or something stronger and tilted the saddle up in the rear. I felt totally comfortable with it this way. I felt even better later when I learned that some racers ride with the saddle this way. It made me think I had the instincts of a champion—or at least that my unorthodox behavior was vindicated.

It's another case of if it feels good, do it. Experiment with your own tilt and see what you like best. If you ride with drop bars, you'll probably end up with an absolutely level saddle position or a slight tilt down in front. If you ride with flat bars, you're more apt to want your saddle tilted up a bit in the front.

There's one caution here. Sometimes when you loosen the under-the-seat nut, you get overenthusiastic and the seat goes all haywire and twists around and then falls off. When this happens, you've got to be certain that you don't get the seat clip on backwards when you reattach. The clip's bolt and nut should be at the back of the seat, not the front. If you put the bolt at the front, the seat will end up too close to the handlebars and you'll desperately conclude that it's impossible to ever get your seat as far from the handlebars as you want it.

Once on a Sierra Club bike tour one of the riders was so miserably uncomfortable that she had to keep stopping for relief. On one of the stops when we were all clustering around to try to give succor, I discovered her problem was a backwards seat clip which pushed her seat toward the handlebars resulting in a scrunch of discomfort. We turned it around and she rode happily ever after—at least on that particular tour.

Incidentally, if you have a very expensive seat post, it will not have a clip with a nut. It will be what is called the cradle type. You'll find two bolts up under the seat for adjusting the tilt. And you won't ever have this backwards problem.

HANDLEBARS: If you can't bring your saddle into the proper relation with the handlebars without totally lousing up its relation to the center of the crank hanger, then you'll need to make your adjustment by getting a longer or shorter handlebar stem. (There are also adjustable handlebar stems available.)

Your handlebar height should be about the same as your seat height. Make the top of the handlebars even with the front of the saddle. Again be sure to leave enough stem inside the down tube; 2½ inches is the recommended amount.

Learning Ride from Wrong

STOP BEFORE YOU START: Your 10-speed bike will have hand-controlled caliper brakes like a motorcycle, but you may be learning to ride on a clunker with coaster brakes. Coasters, remember, are operated with the feet, not the hands. You simply stomp the pedals backwards to slow or stop.

With caliper brakes usually the left-hand lever controls the front brake and the right-hand lever the rear brake (but be sure to check the bike you're riding). The reason for the prevalence of the left-rear, right-front pattern is, I suppose, that most of us are right-handed. If you hit one brake harder than the other or faster than the other or even alone without the other, that one should be your rear brake. You're less likely to flip yourself with the rear brake. I hasten to affirm that this is my opinion. As always, there's an opposite view that claims the flipping problem occurs mostly when you apply the rear brake alone. In this case, the majority opinion *is* on my side.

To me, the logical and soundest method of braking is always to squeeze both levers simultaneously, at least until you've gotten the feel of the bike you're riding. Different brakes on different bikes have totally different stopping characteristics. Only experience with the particular bike you're riding can make your braking safe. The better the bike, the more cautiously should you squeeze the levers when becoming familiar with the braking.

It's a funny thing, but on bicycles it can be just as dangerous to stop quickly as to stop too slowly. The panic stop can be disastrous. This is because a bike has a short wheelbase and the bike and rider together have a high center of gravity. When you slam on the brakes so hard that the front wheel locks, you suddenly reduce the weight over the rear wheel and you get rear wheel skid, or even worse, you find yourself being pitched headfirst over the handlebars. It is very important to practice stopping until you know how to execute a fast stop without losing control of the bike.

Pitchover is more likely to happen on fast downhill runs. To help avoid it, if you have to stop suddenly when going downhill, move back on the seat as far as you can. This changes the center of gravity to your advantage and puts more weight on the rear wheel, where you need it. Incidentally, the correct braking technique for downhill riding is to apply and release the brakes in spurts—on, off—on, off—just as is recommended for cars. This keeps the pads from overheating and wearing out. I've seen brake pads worn totally concave after one ride by a heavy rider on a route with a lot of downhill.

In order to lessen the danger of pitchover, especially for beginning cyclists, I've heard some biking experts even go so far as to advocate adjusting the front brake so that it can't be slammed on in a panic stop. The front caliper's grip on the rim is adjusted so loosely that no matter how hard you squeeze the lever, the brake can't clamp on and "freeze" the wheel. It can only slow it down. The rear caliper is kept in normal stopping adjustment. Although this system decreases your total braking effectiveness, it can help prevent skids and pitchovers. You have to analyze your cycling—and your psyche—to see which is more important to you.

Bike Riding for People Who Don't Know How to Ride a Bike

RIDING FOR A FALL: It's scary to start out riding a bike, if you've never ridden one and you're old enough and wise enough to know what happens to bones and teeth and other cherished bodily parts when they hit hard surfaces. You also are worried about smashing up your lovely brand-new bike. Your fears cause you to tense up, and tensed up is exactly what you shouldn't be when you're in fresh hot pursuit of elusive balance.

Now, while it's impossible to eliminate the quite legitimate and justifiable fear that you're going to fall, you can at least eliminate the fear of smashing your big two-wheel investment. The way you do this is simple. You don't ride your new bike. You find yourself a clunker or, in modern parlance, a trashmo. You might borrow it from a friend who has had it moldering in his garage for years and doesn't care what happens to it.

You might buy one at a garage sale or tag sale or whatever they call them in your area. If the price is low enough, you can't lose, because you can always sell it again or give it away to a charitable organization and take a tax deduction.

If neither of these possibilities is open to you, you can always (shhhhhhh!) rent a bike to learn on. If your conscience begins to nibble at you, you can pick and choose and come up with the rattiest bike in the place.

Whichever of these bike procurement methods you decide to go with, don't worry if your particular trashmo is not a 10-speed. In fact, you're better off if it isn't, because then you won't have the gears to fuss with and can concentrate all your efforts on acquiring balance.

Don't worry about the frame size either, except don't get one larger than your correct size. In this case the smaller the frame, the better, because the closer you are to the ground, the better.

If you're a man, don't worry about the gender of your bicycle. You'd actually be much better off learning on a woman's frame. That crossbar is a cross you can happily do without bearing as you make your first faltering pedalings.

HANDS OFF: Before we go into how you should handle your learning experience, I'd like to mention the one way you shouldn't. Don't have a friend grip the back of your saddle and simultaneously push you and hold you up, the way you always see it done in those warm little pictures of Daddy teaching Junior or Junioress how to ride his/her bike. This method of teaching may explain why you see so many kids running around with scabs on their knees and elbows and missing front teeth.

The hand-on-the-saddle method is fraught with flaws. As an adult you may be too large and heavy for your friend to hold you with one hand. Then, too, you may really get going and your friend won't be able to trot along and keep up with you. You will suddenly find his hand gone and with it goes your confidence. In comes panic to fill the vacuum and it's May Day.

Finally, if your friend is a bike rider, he may have forgotten how it feels not to know how to ride. He'll push you too fast in both senses of the phrase. On the other hand, if the friend is not a bike rider, he'll have not the most remote idea about what you're trying to do and why. You're better off without him, too.

SPACED OUT: Whichever of the following learning methods you use, be sure to use it in some wide-open space that's free from cars. Some good places are a parking lot when the stores or factory it serves are closed or a deserted school playground or your residential streets very early on Sunday mornings. If there's noplace else available to you, you could go up and down your own driveway, although that doesn't give you much elbow and knee thrashing around room.

TRAINING WHEELS: Training wheels (also called balancing wheels) are those two wheels you attach to the rear axle. They are inexpensive and easy to put on. When you ride with training wheels and start to tip over to one side, the training wheel on that side touches the ground and you remain upright. After you've bounced back and forth from training wheel on one side to training wheel on the other side for a while, the theory is that you suddenly discover the laws of balance and you no longer teeter to one side or the other. Your training wheels then hang there uselessly. You remove them and you are a two-wheel bike rider forever after. This theory sometimes works. Sometimes it doesn't.

It can happen that you become too dependent on the training wheels and they become a crutch, as my high school Latin teacher used to claim a pony to translate Caesar was. You feel you can't get along without them and it becomes as hard to kick the training wheels as it is to learn to ride a bike in the first place.

The other hazard with training wheels is that you may turn out to be such a natural-born cyclist that you catch on to how it's done right away. You may be tooling along in perfect balance with the training wheels hanging there like Crazy Guggenheim "not doin' nothin'." Then you come to a corner and, using all the correct instincts of the natural cyclist that you are, you lean into it, slamming down one training wheel, and you proceed to execute a sideways cartwheel. An early-on major splat like this can be demoralizing and may knock the beautiful natural instincts out of you for a while.

Do a little self-analysis and if you decide that training wheels aren't for you, try the next method.

NOSTALGIA TRIP: You are now going to ride back into time. When the modern bicycles weren't even a gleam in Mr. Schwinn's eye, the bicycle didn't have pedals. You just sat there and pushed yourself along with your feet, double scooter style. So take out your handy 6-inch crescent wrench and lower the seat of your two-wheel rattletrap so that when you sit on it you can plant both feet solidly on the ground. Then with the same wrench loosen the nut where each pedal joins the crank and remove the pedals. (The left pedal is loosened by turning the wrench clockwise.)

Now emulate your cycling ancestors. Push yourself along, putting your feet down whenever necessary, even if it's after every push. (If your bike has coaster brakes rather than calipers, you'll have to put your feet down to stop, so don't let yourself get going too fast.) Gradually start coasting a little. Then as you begin to feel your balance taking hold, coast a little farther. When you can coast for several feet at a time, try to coast for several more by coasting down a very small hill. When you can execute this maneuver with élan, stop and put the pedals back on.

Now pedal a couple of strokes and coast. Any time you feel insecure, put your feet down, but be careful you don't whap your ankles with the pedals. Do more and more pedaling between each coasting period and, oh, *mirabile dictu,* you're riding.

Practice a great deal in your empty space before you venture into the streets. Practice making turns in both directions. Practice stopping. If you're riding a 3-speed, practice shifting so you can get the feel of riding in different gears. Remember, with a 3-speed you shift when *not* pedaling. It's exactly the opposite of the 10-speed.

When you've ridden your clunker successfully for about a week, raise the saddle to the proper height (see page 105) and ride it for another week. Then you're ready for the big time, your 10-speed.

As you approach the wonderful machine, if you find you still have stirrings of insecurity, try riding at first with the seat lowered. Then raise it to normal height as soon as your confidence firms up. The goal with this whole overly gradual learning process is for you never to feel beyond your depth, for you always to feel relaxed and at ease with yourself and your bike.

Bike Riding for People Who Know How to Ride a Bike

MONKEY SEE, MONKEY DON'T: Ted Van der Kolk, owner of the Flying Dutchman Bicycle Company in Glendale, California, puts it in his artless Nederlander way, "Most Americans ride bicycles like monkeys." He's got a point there. In fact, he's got a couple of points.

Think of your average monkey riding a bicycle. There he is pedaling along with his knees up around his chin. His toes curl over the front edge of the pedals and he's riding with the pedals underneath his arches.

Now think of your average American cyclist. He,

too, probably has his knees up around his chin, because his seat's too low, and although his toes aren't hanging out of his shoes and they aren't long enough or prehensile enough to curl over the pedals, he clearly is riding with the pedals under his arches.

Since you've already adjusted your saddle to the correct height, you don't have the knee-chin problem. If you want to raise yourself still another notch on the primate scale, look like a pro, and what's really important, cycle the most efficient way, always ride with the ball of your foot on the pedals. (One good thing about toe clips is that with them you *have* to ride with the ball of your foot.)

A WELL-TURNED ANKLE: While we're talking about feet and what they're doing, we might as well consider ankling since you'll be hearing a lot about it. Ankling is the approved pedaling technique. When you ankle, as you might suspect, your ankles come into play. To use time-telling terms, at 12 o'clock your toe is pointed up slightly and at 6 o'clock your toe is pointed down slightly. At all the other positions on the clock, your foot is simply in the process of moving toward the position it will be in at 12 and 6.

Now that you know what ankling is, I advise you to forget it. Not that it shouldn't be done. It should, because it's the most efficient way to pedal. You should forget about it, because if you have your seat at the right height and your feet in the right position on the pedals and you're pedaling in a smooth, non-jerky motion, you're probably going to ankle naturally without even thinking about it.

I find that when I concentrate on ankling, I get all mixed up and find myself engaging in a lot of exaggerated and unproductive and even counterproductive motion which does nothing except give me weary ankles. Conscious ankling is like conscious breathing. (Try doing the latter for a full minute, and you'll see what I mean.)

SHIFTING FOR YOURSELF: The greatest difficulty many new arrivals in the realm of the 10-speed have is with the art of shifting gears. Not understanding the hows or whys of shifting, a lot of them just give up and leave the bike in whatever gear it happened to be in when delivered. This blows all the wonderful advantages of the machine. Intelligence has nothing to do with this. I know a learned Ph.D. from Stanford whose gears must by now be permanently frozen from lack of use. They've never been shifted. (And let's all hope his bike was delivered to him in some middle gear, rather than a 94 or 38.)

If that wonderful shop you've picked out with such care is as wonderful as it should be, they will spend at least a few minutes demonstrating to you the technique of shifting. It's possible, of course, that you've come on with such knowledgeability, chatting about cotterless cranks and double-butted tubing, that the shop owner will think you're an old pro and wouldn't insult you by offering a demonstration. But even if you do get a shop demonstration, it's likely to be so cursory and casual that it won't stick. So we'll go over the whole business step by step.

On a 10-speed bike the shifting lever on your left controls the chainwheel (front) and the one on your right controls the freewheel (back). There are two choices of gears on the front and five on the back. Two times five equals ten, or the sum total of your gear choices. On a 15-speed bike there are three sprockets in front and those in combination with the back five give you three times five, or fifteen gears.

With the chainwheel the small wheel is the lower gear. With the freewheel it's just the opposite: the largest sprocket is the lowest gear. As you pull the left lever toward you, you move from a lower gear to a higher gear. As you pull the right lever toward you, you move from a higher gear to a lower one. It's too bad the levers work the opposite from each other, but they just do. So far, the one exception to this rule is the Suntour front derailleur. With this the higher gear is in the front position and the lower is toward the rider.

TALKING TORQUE: Perhaps we should pause here and discuss the principles behind bicycle gears. I talked to a physics professor for a simple explanation of how they work. (Did you ever try to get a simple explanation out of a physics professor?) Boiled down and filtered for clarification, his analysis was that bicycle gears work basically like a pulley, specifically a differential pulley. When you transmit power from a small wheel to a large wheel, you get a lot of force but little speed. (He called this force torque and I've also heard it called mechanical advantage.) When you transmit power from a large wheel to a small one, you get speed but not much torque.

Therefore, when you have your chain riding on the small sprocket in front (where you're applying pedal power) and the largest sprocket in back, you have the power to climb a hill, but you climb it slowly. Conversely, when the chain is on the large wheel in front and the smallest in back, you can go lickety-split, but you don't have climbing power. The gradations in between your large and small sprockets produce gradations in speed and torque.

8—EASY—8: According to some experts, a 10-speed is really an 8-speed, because you should never, never ride with the chain on the big sprocket in front and the biggest sprocket in back or on the small sprocket in front and the smallest sprocket in back. This is because in these positions the chain runs at an awkward lateral angle, causing it to wear out faster.

I only found out this immortal truth after I had done a lot of riding and had settled on the combination of the small front sprocket and the smallest back sprocket as my all-time favorite gear. Not wanting to give it up, I talked it over with Larry Branson. As always, he had a pragmatic approach. "If it isn't dragging or scraping, it's probably okay. The really bad combination is the large wheel and the large wheel. That's where the chain has to stretch the most." Since my chain neither dragged nor scraped when I rode small and small, I decided to keep using this gear, although I do try not to ride in it quite as much as I did before.

PLAYING THE NUMBERS: Some people like to give their gears numbers—1st, 2nd, 3rd, etc., all the way up to 10th. If you're obsessed by a desire to call every gear by such a sequence name, you can figure it thusly. First is the lowest gear (small chainwheel with biggest freewheel sprocket) and 10th is the highest (large chainwheel with smallest freewheel sprocket). For 2nd, 3rd, 4th, and 5th, still on the small chainwheel, you shift down to the second largest freewheel sprocket, the third largest next, etc., until you get to the smallest, which is 5th gear.

For gears 6, 7, 8, 9, and 10 you shift the front derailleur and get the chain onto the large chainwheel sprocket. Sixth gear is a combination of the large chainwheel and the largest freewheel sprocket. (This gear, incidentally, is the forbidden one.) For 7th, 8th, 9th, and 10th you shift over to the second largest freewheel sprocket, to the third largest, etc., until you get to the smallest sprocket, which is 10th gear.

One thing that makes this method of counting gears particularly confusing is that in the middle gears they don't really go in order from lowest to highest. For example, my 4th gear is actually higher than my 6th, 7th or 8th:

		14	17	22	28	34
Gear ratios	52	100.3	82.6	63.8	50.1	41.3
	39	75.2	61.9	47.9	37.6	31.0

		14	17	22	28	34
Gear numbers	52	10th	9th	8th	7th	6th
	39	5th	4th	3rd	2nd	1st

The only use I can see for this system is to say to a repairman, for instance, "I get a dragging noise in 5th gear. Can you eliminate this?" This way you both know exactly which gear you're talking about.

Some experienced cyclists prefer to number gears as they actually run according to their ratios. Although the highest will still be the large chainwheel sprocket and the smallest freewheel sprocket, and the lowest will still be the small in front and the largest in back, in the middle gears you will sometimes have to go back and forth between the large and small wheel in front as you count your gears up or down.

The trouble with this method becomes apparent when you're talking gears with another cyclist or the mechanic. You find you don't have a common point of orientation. For example, the location of your 8th gear can and probably will be different from the location of somebody else's 8th.

Ted Van der Kolk calls all this gear numbering nonsense. He claims there's no such thing as 1st, 2nd, 3rd, etc. I must admit that I find numbering the gears only confuses me. I prefer to think of them in terms of their ratios, because that's what really tells you something. As I mentioned before, it's a great help to have your gear ratios typed and taped to your handlebars.

GETTING THE KNACK: Two important things to remember when you shift a 10-speed. First and foremost, you can *only* shift when you're pedaling. Otherwise, the chain's not moving and can't possibly peel off one sprocket and onto the next. Not only do you get no shifting action, but you can damage the cable, the derailleur, the chain, the cogs, or maybe everything all at once. This shifting when pedaling can be especially hard to remember if you have any experience with a 3-speed, because with those you can only shift when you're *not* pedaling. Caution: If after you're accustomed to your 10-speed and its shifting vagaries and you borrow or rent a 3-speed, be sure to keep your wits about you at all times. If you shift one of those while pedaling, you can cream the gears to a fare-thee-well, and it's a very expensive proposition to get them made right again.

There's an addendum to this shift-a-10-speed-only-while-pedaling edict. Although you should be pedaling when you shift, you shouldn't be pedaling with great force. You shouldn't, for example, be pedaling with all leg and lung up a hill and then decide you'd like to go for a lower gear. The chain resists moving off the cogs when you're under full power and the derailleur is put under strain.

Ten-speed biking is the thinking person's sport. You have to plan ahead if you want to shift down. And yet not too far ahead. If you see a hill coming and think, "I'll get ready for that rascal," and drop down to something in the low 30's, you will suddenly find yourself spinning your pedals, losing all momentum. Only time and experience will tell you when the golden moment of downshifting arrives, but you will get the knack of it with trial and error. Once you do, it will be with you all your cycling days.

The second important caution about shifting is never to do it when pedaling backwards. (Why are you doing that, anyway?) This is hard to remember if you were raised on coaster brakes and instinctively want to slam your feet backwards for a stop. Do this and you risk throwing the chain off the chainwheel and destroying your derailleur.

If by some happenstance you should ever throw your chain, then again to quote the Erasmus of Cycling, Mynheer Van der Kolk, "Keep smiling, keep relaxed. Just put on your brakes, get off your bike, and put the chain back on." Putting the chain back on is no big deal. You simply pull back the derailleur body. This releases the tension of the chain and makes it possible for you to return the chain to the appropriate sprocket of the chainwheel. Be sure it *is* the appropriate sprocket, that is to say, the one it was on when it came off, or your gear lever will be in the wrong position. Remember, unless it's a Suntour derailleur, if the left lever is in the forward position, the chain goes on the small chainwheel sprocket. If the lever is toward you, the chain goes on the large one.

MUSIC TO YOUR GEARS: It takes a lot of practice to shift with ease and skill. It's rather like playing the violin in that you have to develop a feel as to where a certain note, or in this case, a certain gear is. Naturally, chainwheel shifting isn't as difficult as freewheel shifting, because you have only two positions to worry about. But with the five to contend with on the freewheel, that's another matter.

Incidentally, if you feel you'll never be able to get the knack of playing gears like a violin, you can play them more like a piano if you put the new Shimano Positron derailleur on your bike. With the Positron you only have to give the shifting lever a slight nudge and the derailleur takes over and clicks you into the next gear. I haven't tried the Positron myself, but according to the somewhat biased folks at Shimano, it takes the human error out of shifting.

Smart people shift their rear derailleur only one step at a time. It's not recommended to flip from the lowest gear on the freewheel to the highest, unless you have no regard at all for the health of your chain or you enjoy having it jam or derail. Going a step at a time is even more important while you're getting the feel of the gears. Slowly, firmly, carefully, e-a-s-e your lever to the next step, almost the same way you're advised to slowly squeeze the trigger of a gun, if you go for that sort of thing.

When I was first shifting gears, I evolved the clunk and jingle theory. I found that if the gear made a clunking sound, I hadn't quite moved the shifting lever far enough. If it jingled, I had moved it a hair too far and needed to nudge it back a bit. This may work for you or you may hit upon some new formula peculiar to your gears and their sounds.

Then when you have the whole business of gear shifting in hand, you can fall prey to another sin that Ted Van der Kolk finds in us Yankee simian cyclists. We tend to get gear happy. He claims to have seen one fellow shift gears five times in one city block, one *flat* city block. Hardly necessary and it keeps one's hand off the handlebars more than necessary and is therefore a minor safety hazard. It's also tiring on the legs when you keep changing gears all the time. As the stoic philosopher says, "Moderation in all things." (And as the hedonist adds, "Including moderation.")

RIDING HIGH: Now that you know how to shift, the question is what gears are best to ride in? No easy answer here. Generally, low gears are for uphill, high are for downhill, and medium are for medium terrain. But actually the gear you choose depends on a number of other factors as well: your condition, the road's condition, the weather's condition (primarily, is it windy?), and the speed you're going.

One thing we can say about gears, however. Most cyclists, especially most male cyclists, tend to ride in a gear that's too high. As automotive expert Tom Mc-Cahill says in *Mechanix Illustrated*, "Most of our would-be he-man riders insist on using gearing too high for the occasion and lose a lot of the fun and quite a bit of the exercise."

I've talked to a number of men about the gears they ride in and several have said with a glint of pride, "Oh, I just keep it in my highest gear all the time." I'll admit that in my first 10-speed days I, too, always rode in too high a gear, not the highest I had but still higher than I had any business in. I don't think I did this out of a try for machismo, although who knows what kind of subconscious motivations a woman has in these days of lib and feminism? I *think* my idea was that I got more exercise, if I rode in a high gear and huffed and puffed a lot. I'd be burning up more calories and become fashionably gaunt. This approach I later found out was all wrong. The best exercise, at least for the cardiovascular system, comes from more pedal rotations. This keeps those leg muscles squeezing those blood vessels and shooting the cranberry juice of life back to the heart.

Another possible motivation for pulling a high gear is the old Puritan ethic, which still lurks in our bones, though we may have fleshed them over with easy living. We have the subconscious notion that if it hurts, it's good for us; if it's hard work, it will pedal us into the kingdom of heaven.

But whatever the goal—machismo, physical conditioning, or kingdom of heaven—high-gear pushing is not the way to get there.

PEDAL TALK: One way of selecting a gear that's not too high for you is to use one that allows you to ride at a conversational pace. This is something runners and sometimes racing cyclists in training do. It's equally effective for the average adult bike rider who wants to bike the no-sweat, no-strain way. The conversational pace is exactly what it says. It's the speed at which you can ride and still carry on a conversation without getting winded and breathless.

Start off, if you're on the flat, in a gear in the 60's and chat away. Talk to yourself if there's no one else around, or if you prefer, you can sing. If you find you have plenty of wind and you feel as if you're spinning your pedals, move up a gear. If you find yourself gasping, move down a gear. Keep changing gears until you find the perfect conversational cadence. If you go up a hill, you'll have to drop down a gear or two to keep the conversation going. When you descend, you can go into a higher gear and still not interrupt the conversation.

You'll find that the more you ride and the better shape you get into, the higher gear you can talk in.

CADENCE COUNT: What you're doing with this conversational approach is establishing your proper cadence. Once you've established that, you can always pedal with about the same number of strokes per minute. You use your gears to help you keep that cadence going at all times. 1—2—3—4—5, up comes a hill and you shift down 1—2—3—4—5. Your feet keep making the same number of revolutions per minute, but you just don't go as far with each revolution. Your speed decreases, but your effort remains the same.

You top the hill and start down the other side, shifting to a high gear, still pedaling 1—2—3—4—5, but you now go farther with each stroke and hence your speed picks up. You reach the flat. You shift to a middle gear 1—2—3—4—5. All the while you're putting forth the same effort, but your speed has varied, thanks to your gears.

I know that keeping the same pedaling speed is the scientifically sound way to ride. I know you get the most miles for your energy expenditure this way. But I can't bring myself to do it. At least, not all the time. I like to pedal like fury for a while and then coast. My greatest joy comes when I can get a lot of momentum going and actually coast uphill for a few yards. I feel I'm really putting something over on the laws of physics.

I also have the idea that I get less tired when I vary my cadence and throw in a few coasts. I learned from ski touring that if you vary the rhythm of your stride, your muscles have a chance to recover and you get a second muscular wind. Now, while this may not hold true for cycling—and it probably doesn't, since keeping the same cadence is one of the few points everyone seems to agree on—in my kinesthetic heart I still feel it does. So vary my pace I always do. Another reason and possibly it's the main one that I don't 1—2—3—4—5 all the time, is that I find it boring. If there's one thing I don't want to do with a delightful activity like biking, it is to cast a pall of boredom over it.

TAKING A STAND: Honking in bikese means really giving it your all by standing up on the pedals and straining for all you're worth or think you're worth. Honking is used on steep hills. But beware. You are pouring all your physical force into a weak vessel, your knee. A nurse cyclist once told me that if you have any history of knee trouble, this much pressure on an inherently not-too-well-constructed joint can cause severe trouble and may put you out of riding commission, among other commissions.

Standing up some is good for you, though. This is true when you're riding over rough surfaces—bumps, holes, etc. Rising up off the saddle prevents spine-jarring, something no one needs. Actually your self-preservation instincts will probably pull you up off the seat in such circumstances, but I just thought I'd better mention it, in case your instincts let you down.

PERPENDICULAR POSITION: Your instincts may let you down in another situation. They will have you leaning into a turn. This is the right thing for them to do, unless you're making a turn on a surface that has sand or gravel or oil or some other delightful skid-inducing product on it. I've seen enough kids picking gravel from their knees to give me a healthy respect for taking suspect turns straight up rather than on the rocks.

CAUGHT IN THE DRAFT: Members of cycling clubs who ride together a lot often indulge in a practice called drafting. This means the riders ride in a line close behind each other. As a result every rider except No. 1 is riding in a pocket of low wind resistance and the riding takes much less effort. By taking turns as leader so that no one person has to bear the brunt of the wind for too long, the group can travel farther and faster than they normally could.

It's easy to see the dangers inherent in drafting. Unskilled or even semi-skilled cyclists can get themselves in some truly glorious pile-ups by drafting. I really don't recommend it until you have a great deal of riding experience under your wheels. And never, never try it with a bunch of cyclists who don't know what they're doing.

I have a friend who makes me furious by drafting

behind me when she feels like taking it easy for a while. I know she doesn't have the skill to execute a tricky evasive action should it become necessary. I know her brakes aren't as good as mine. And what is worse, I know that about half the time she isn't paying any attention to what she's doing. She's just drafting and dreaming. No matter how often I lecture her on tailgating, every once in a while I find her front tire starting to nuzzle up to my rear one. I try to be philosophical about it, because she's a fairly pleasant cycling companion, aside from this one bad habit. But I always try to remember to bring along my Blue Cross card.

INCENTIVE PLAN: Reading about bicycling can only do so much for you. The only way to really develop cycling skills is by experience. If you're an intelligent, sentient, adult human being, the more you ride, the better you'll ride, evolving effective bicycling methods of your own.

All you need to do is get up and go; *regularly* get up and go. You may find, however, that you have an initial lethargy to overcome. Lethargy is that small sluggish voice that tells you you're too tired or it's too cold or too hot or too windy or, well, you know all the possible excuses for not going out and doing something.

Happily there is a way to break this sloth barrier. Sign up to earn a Presidential Sports Award in bicycling. Here's how it works. Write to Presidential

Sports Award, 400 6th Street, S.W., Washington, D.C. 20201. They will send you a logbook and a list of the qualifying standards. The standards for the award in bicycling are:

1. Bicycle a minimum of 600 miles (more than five gears); or bicycle a minimum of 400 miles (five or fewer gears).
2. No more than 12 miles in any one day may be credited to total (more than five gears); no more than 8 miles in any one day may be credited to total (five or fewer gears).
3. Requirements must be completed within four months.

You have to be over eighteen to participate, but for us that's no problem.

As you can see, this program is hardly arduous. It's designed to get you out on your bike regularly and to keep you from popping an aneurysm on a weekend sports binge. Note, however, that these distances are just the maximum you can count. You can go as many extra uncountable miles as you choose. Incidentally, unlike most things coming out of Washington, Presidential Sports Awards work strictly on the honor system.

By the time you've finished the program, you're certain to be a competent cyclist and that will be a better reward than the flashy jacket emblem, the discrete lapel pin, and the framable certificate you receive in recognition of your accomplishment.

chapter 7

OPTIONAL EXTRAS

Accessories After the Fact

After previously virtually suggesting that you sell your first-born to the gypsies to get the money to buy the best bike imaginable, I have to backpedal a little now. Don't use up every last morsel of your discretionary income on the bicycle itself, because there are a number of accessories that are vital to your full enjoyment of the bike. Spending all your money on the bike and having nothing left for its embellishments is like buying a lovely new home and leaving nothing for furniture or landscaping.

But don't swing too far the other way either. There is no end to the amount of junk you can hang on a bike and no end to the manufacturers who are thinking up new stuff "vital to your cycling pleasure and safety." Resist as much of this paraphernalia as you can. Make it like the rule of the smorgasbord: take all you want, but use all you take. Remember, everything weighs something. There's little point to investing in a 23-pound bike and loading it up with 12 pounds' worth of miscellaneous unused accessories. (Of course, you're still better off than you would be doing the same thing with a 35-pound bike.)

LOCKS: Rick Lipski, owner of the Cyclery in Chicago, won't even sell a bike without a lock. This isn't hard to understand, since in Chicago three out of every five new bikes sold are eventually stolen. We'll go into the kinds of locks available in Chapter 9, but you can figure on setting aside from $10 to $15 for this item. This is not so much an accessory as an insurance policy.

KICKSTAND: On the less expensive bikes a kickstand comes already attached. On the more expensive bikes you have to add it yourself (under $5). Strangely enough, this innocuous little utilitarian item is another point of controversy in biking circles. Purists won't have anything to do with kickstands, because they say they add weight to the bike—and low-down weight at that—they mar the surface where they're attached, they're likely to come loose and flop around, and they don't work, anyway, since with the slightest breeze or nudge over goes the bike.

All probably true, but still I like a kickstand.

There's not always someplace to lean a bike, and if there is, the someone in charge of the someplace doesn't like you to lean it there. He thinks you'll scratch up his wall or injure his tree. I don't like laying my bike on the ground or sidewalk, either. It can get mucked up or a person can get mucked up tripping over it.

I don't find that my bike falls over very often with a kickstand, because my kickstand is the right length. When I first got my latest bike it used to continually do a dead tree topple and hit the deck for no apparent reason. I was idly grousing about this tendency to my bike shop man. He looked at the kickstand and said, "No wonder. It's too long." He pointed out some little marks along the side of the stand. These indicate where you should slice it off to make it the right length for the frame size. I ride a 19-inch frame and the kickstand was the length for a 24-inch frame. A quick snicker-snack and I never had the topple problem again.

The most common light-alloy brand of kickstand is the ESGE by Pletscher, which unfortunately has cutting marks in metric. (The 270 mark is correct for a 21-inch frame.) Some stands have a sliding leg for adjustment. If you're purchasing your own stand, be sure to mention your frame size, as some manufacturers have different models for different frame sizes.

TIRE PUMP: Actually you should have two tire pumps: one for home and one for the road. The road one, which snaps onto the frame, frequently comes with the bike.

Why can't you just use the one for the road all the time and forget buying the home model? Mainly because you will reduce yourself to a state of exhaustion before you even start riding if you attempt to pump up your tires to the proper state of hard with the road pump. The road pump is actually only designed for fixing flats in an emergency. All you're supposed to do is firm up the tire sufficient unto getting you to where you can really pump it up with an effective pump.

There's the big clue word for your home pump, *effective*. In an unnatural fit of thrift I first bought the cheapest tire pump (around $1.50) I could find in the local auto supply store. It was the kind you screw onto the tire valve. Not only was this false bargain practically as hard to pump and slow to fill as the road model, but every time I tried to unscrew it to check the tire pressure, I lost about a third of the air I had put in. Checking the pressure with one of those little hand gauges let out a little more air.

Next I invested in a slightly more expensive pump ($3.50). This was at least from a bicycle shop, but it wasn't easy to pump either, and I still had to use the tire gauge. I did, though, appreciate the fact that it was clipped on by pressing a lever (thumbblock) and didn't let out 20 pounds of air every time I took it off the valve. I was fairly content with this pump for about three months. Then it gradually flamed out on me. I'd pump and pump, but most of the time it seemed to have no pressure at all. The handle just clunked down with no resistance. And of course, no air was going into the tire.

Finally I gave up. I clomped into a bike shop and plunked down around $16.50 for the best pump they had in stock. It was a Raymar (Raleigh dealer) high-pressure pump with a built-in pressure gauge. It's a gem. It's sturdy. It pumps easily and quickly. All I have to do is watch the needle on the gauge and stop when it gets into the green zone (60–65 pounds pressure). When I disattach it from the tire valve, there's a hissing sound of air but it's not air escaping from the tire. It's only air that was in the pump. There's an adapter to make it possible for the pump to fit the Presta valve of the higher pressure sew-ups. (If I ever do succumb to their siren lure, I'll be ready to do the frequent—read constant—pumping they require.)

Schwinn also makes an excellent high-pressure tire pump with a gauge. If your bike shop doesn't have one of these topnotch pumps, either have them order one for you or go somewhere else. Accept no substitutes!

HORNS AND BELLS: There are two reasons to have some kind of sound maker on your bike: the altruistic and the egocentric. The altruistic sound maker is to protect pedestrians who might stroll into your path, and the egocentric is to protect you from cars that might unwittingly bash you. Any kind of tinkling bell or small beep horn will take care of the former, but

when a car has its windows rolled up, its air condi-
tioner roaring, its radio blaring, it takes something in
the nature of an air-raid siren to get through.

Possibly Super Sound would work for you. This is
an aerosol sound maker you attach to your handlebars. It's piercing, man, piercing. When you shoot it
off, it sounds as if someone has just run over a ban-
shee. It's a sound that should at least do something to
a driver—startle him into immobility or possibly
cause him to spurt forward in nervous reaction.

The problem with Super Sound is that while protecting you from mashing, it plays hell with your
aural cilia. If you inflict too much hell on them, eventually your hearing is adversely affected. This is what
happens to motorcyclists who subject their ears to the
relentless unmuffled roar of their machines. (And it
couldn't happen to a more deserving group.) At any
rate, if you do decide on Super Sound, be sure to
follow the directions and just punch down in short
blasts so as to protect your tender cilia.

In lieu of mechanical devices like a horn or bell or
Super Sound, screaming and shouting often work if
you have good projection. Screams and shouts also
have the great cycle accessory advantages of light
weight and unstealability.

MIRRORS: The best device a cyclist could have for
riding safety would be eyes in the back of his head.
Another set on each side would be a help, too. Since
these accessories aren't available at most bike shops,

how about rear-view mirrors? Although there are cyclists who have found them to be things of safety and
joys forever, I've never cared for them, mainly because I don't like projecting metal anythings on my
bike.

Handlebar rear-view mirrors are difficult to keep in
adjustment, the nature of the bike being that it jiggles
things loose. If you have to constantly remove one
hand from the handlebars to adjust a mirror, the
safety advantage is dubious. I don't find the tiny mirrors you attach to your glasses or cap too effective, either. It's hard to focus on a precise threat behind you
and then there's the danger of its sticking out in front
of you.

Actually it's best if you can just train yourself to
glance quickly over your left shoulder without un-
consciously turning your wheel to the left in the process. (Believe me, this takes some training.)

The other recommended way of seeing behind,
especially when you're riding with drop handlebars,
is to duck your head down and peer backwards just
beneath your armpit. I'm still working on this one. I
have trouble orienting myself to the semi-upside-
down image, but I think that once mastered, this is
going to prove to be the best method.

REAR RACK: A rear rack is the kind you attach to your
back axle and carry things on. It's called a rear rack,
because there are other racks used to support handlebar bags and they go up front. The rack is made of

light alloy or steel or a combination of the two. The price ranges from $5 to around $11. Some are protected with a vinyl coating (Wheeling Dervish). Pletscher is inexpensive and the easiest to find in bike shops, but the other brands are equally good. Among the recommended ones are Karrimor, and TC (Touring Cyclist).

Some racks have a spring clamp that you can lift up and anchor things under (like a windbreaker or a sweater or the evening paper). If the rack you choose doesn't have a clamp, as some of the lighter-weight, designed-for-touring models don't, you should get two or three of those elastic cords with hooks on the end to hold things onto your rack. These are known as stretch cords, sandows, bongis or Bungees. In fact, you should get a few of these no matter what kind of rack you buy, because they're very handy for all bicycling purposes. Be sure to buy at least two or three different lengths. They run from about 8 inches to 30 inches.

Not the least of uses of stretch cords is for my own original unpatented rack pack. In biking circles those two saddlebags that you hang over the back rack are called panniers in the French manner. I call my invention *la boîte* to give it a little class, too. It needs all the class it can get. To call a box a box, my *boîte* is a toaster box.

Here's how you assemble *la boîte*. Go to the nearest appliance store and con them out of a box that a toaster came in. Take the box and punch holes near the bottom edge on either side and on each end. Run a stretch cord through each set of holes, one across and one end to end. Then attach the hooks to the bike rack, and you have yourself a sturdily attached, capacious container that can hold just about all you'll need to have with you on a day ride and still have room for the fruits of minor shopping.

La boîte is the perfect size and shape to fit on the rack. It is extremely lightweight. The lid-making sides can be left up to increase the depth of the box. In that case, a jacket or sweater spread over the top and held in place by still another stretch cord will seal in the contents. Incidentally, a shoe box with a lid also makes a tidier but tinier *boîte*.

You can make *la boîte* look a little more elegant by covering it with sticky-backed decorative paper or washable contact shelf paper. I don't think any of this fancying up is necessary, though. There's something appealing to a perverse sense of humor about a fancy 10-speed bike with a brown cardboard box emblazoned Proctor-Silex riding proudly on the rack.

BAGS: If your sense of humor doesn't run to the perverse and you prefer to keep your bike looking more like Robert Redford in "The Great Gatsby" than like Dustin Hoffman in "Midnight Cowboy," then you should carry your necessities in something more elegant.

The TC Daytripper (11 inches x 4½ inches x 4½ inches) is the rich man's *boîte*. It has a zipper running around three sides and is made of bright red or royal blue waterproof nylon duck. It costs around $12.

Another possibility would be one of the many and varied nylon bags. These come in reds, oranges, yellows and blues, so you can match your bike's décor or use the bag as an aid for catching the eye of motorists who tend to be oblivious of a bicyclist's existence. According to the Japanese, yellow is the caution color because it, rather than the traditional red of the Western world, is more easily seen by the human eye. I personally think that day-glo orange grabs the eye even more than yellow. (And here I am riding around with a blue bag that everyone agrees blends totally into the scenery.)

Nylon bags, by the way, are much lighter than the previously popular leather or canvas ones. They're also more waterproof and, of course, more expensive.

There are only slight variations between the major brands—Bellwether, Cannondale, Karrimor, Gerry, Hubbard, Medalist, and TC. You might as well compare prices and just buy the least expensive brand that your shop stocks. It's not worth running around looking for a certain one, considering the subtle differences involved.

Many of these bags, especially those that hang from the saddle, have some kind of flexible styrofoam stiffening insert to keep the bag from going limp as a deflated balloon when it's not fully packed. These are very necessary, yet very rotten to use, because they keep slipping around, blocking the opening into which you want to stick your hand. There's room here for an inventive mind to come up with something better. Watch bike shops and catalogs of accessories for further developments.

Your big decision on bags will be related to how much you want to carry and where you want the weight. Ideally the weight you carry should be equally distributed between the front and the back of the bike. My preference, however, is to keep more weight in the rear, because I find that weight hanging from the handlebars tends to shift around and pull me in directions I don't want to go. It seems to give the handlebars a mind of their own, sometimes with ideas contrary to mine.

If you carry only the sub-basics on your rides, then you can probably get away with a very small saddlebag like the smallest Cannondale or Bellwether, which is a semi-cylinder about 9 inches wide and 5 inches deep. A bag this small, however, condemns you to never carrying lovely little extras like a lunch and a bottle of wine or never picking up some interesting something in a shop you pass on the way. It even eliminates carrying a camera much larger than a Rollei 35 and even that will be a squeeze. The next size up (13 inches long, 6 inches wide, 7 inches deep) is made by Karrimor.

Handlebar bags generally come larger than seat packs. The one made by Bellwether is just about the perfect size for carrying everything you need for a day trip. The zipper compartment can be puffed out to around 10 inches x 12 inches if you really jam stuff in. On top of—or rather outside—that there is a separate Velcro-closed pocket about 6 inches x 5 inches x 2½ inches for things like money and keys and suntan lotion and a camera that you might want to get to fast and frequently. Packed to capacity, though, this handlebar bag really does to me in a big way what I mentioned handlebar bags do to me. Consequently, I occasionally do what I'm sure the Bellwether Company would growl or at least sniff at. I use the handlebar bag as a saddlebag. I run the top straps through the slots in the saddle designed for saddlebag straps and I wrap the bottom strap around the rear rack. Because of its back stiffening, the bag leans at an angle from saddle to rack. It looks funny and occasionally when it's packed to the gills my legs bump it a little as I ride, but I still feel it works better for me than having it in front and always feeling that the handlebars are on the verge of being wrenched from my hands.

If you decide you'd prefer to use the handlebar bag where it belongs, you may need—as I do—a carrying rack for it. This slips over the handlebars in a confusing way that is reminiscent of those take-apart linked nail puzzles. Once on, the rack both holds the bag away from the top-of-the-handlebars brake levers and keeps the bag from drooping down and rubbing a wheel. (This is a special hazard on the smaller frame sizes.) The rack I especially favor is vinyl-coated at the neck so as not to scratch your handlebars. It's called E-Z On E-Z Off, is made by the Park Tool Company, and costs around $4. Bellwether furnishes one with its bag, but it's pretty flimsy and doesn't work well on smaller frames.

When I want to carry a big load, I use a combination of saddlebag and handlebar bag, stuffing as much as possible in the saddlebag in order to carry as little as possible on the handlebars.

An alternative to the saddlebag and handlebar bag for those who like to tote and pick up more than most is the Bellwether rear touring pack. It's a pannier setup that you hang over your rack and fasten to the supports that run from the rack to the axle. If the truth were known—and it probably is—this is actually two handlebar bags sewn together via a wide strip of fabric. You can see by that how much it can hold—enough for a weekend jaunt if you're a compact packer.

There are all kinds of giant touring bag setups, including, for example, rear panniers about twice as big as the above like Bellwether's grand touring pack. There are even front panniers. These are for those of you who progress from casual day-tripping to intensive and fanatic touring-and-camping-out trips. This irrational behavior can happen unexpectedly to the best of people. I even get twinges of longing for it myself, although so far I've been able to fight them off. If you go down this rocky, chuckhole strewn path, the most thorough discussion of packs to meet this kind of cycling need can be found in *Two Wheel Travel: Bicycle Camping and Touring* (Dell).

BACKPACKS: A very poor alternative to bags that you hang on your bike are packs that you hang on your back. Not only are these terribly uncomfortable and fatiguing to wear when you're cycling, but they put the weight way up in the middle of the air where it can throw you off balance. They don't do much toward making you aerodynamically streamlined, either.

I have only heard one person speak favorably of cycling with a backpack. His praise was mainly of one feature: when you get off the bike and go into a store or restroom, you don't have to rummage around in your bike bag to sort out your valuables and take them along, lest they be ripped off. And of course it's also true that there are those who even steal not-so-valuables, including the bag itself that you leave on an untended bike. Still, a backpack's disadvantages outweigh this one advantage for any but very short trips.

If you're inseparably wed to backpacks, though, you may want to check into a special stainless steel rack designed especially to carry a backpack on a bicycle. It's called the Bikepacker. It weighs 19 ounces and costs about $15. (Available from The Bikepacker, P.O. Box 153, Alta Loma, CA 91701.)

WATER BOTTLE: There are many different bottles available for carrying on the frame of the bike in a bottle cage. Some are the thermos variety to keep liquids hot or cold. Some are stainless steel, but most are plastic. The best-known brand is T.A., which supplies the Tour de France racers.

I have a plastic one with a hole in the lid. I like this because I can use it to squirt kamakaze dogs in the face. It would work better as a dog repellent if it had a few drops of ammonia mixed with the water, but then that wouldn't do much for the taste of the water. That taste isn't much to begin with—after riding around in the bottle it becomes reminiscent of old inner tubes. As a matter of fact, a soupçon of peppermint extract does much to make the water more palatable.

You may think a water bottle is unnecessary unless you go in for intensive touring. Not so. Dr. Eugene Gaston recommends that when you cycle in hot weather you should drink a quarter of a bottle's worth every 15 or 20 minutes. Even if you aren't keeping up much of a pace, you need a slug at least every half hour to replenish your vital juices.

Just in case you're curious, the sprinkler top that comes with some water bottles is for when you're racing along at a fast clip in hot weather and want to cool off. If you're riding in a very hot place and the water in your bottle heats up to the air temperature or beyond, drinking it can do more harm than good. Better to lower your body temperature by sprinkling the water on your head and thereby turning your head into an evaporative cooler. Still better for keeping cool is to avoid riding for long periods in intense heat.

LIGHTS: Because of proliferating safety regulations every bicycle now seems to be a virtual rolling reflector system. This certainly makes bikes far more seeable at night, but still doesn't solve the cyclist's problem of seeing where he's going. If you go in for night riding—and some of us don't—you should buy a light.

First, a couple of *not* recommendeds. My most not recommended is a generator set. These attach to the fork. When night falls you move them against the rim so that the turning of the wheel generates the power to make the light shine. There's no battery to wear out and there is something satisfying about creating your own power in an age of energy crisis. But here's the flaw: the generator wheel makes a drag on your wheel. If you're like me, you feel you're suddenly pulling a log in your wake. And unless you pedal hard and fast, you only generate a very dim light. Also, the generator set is always there on your bike contributing excess ounces day or night. The only real advantage I can think of to this kind of light is that if it's the only one you have, you're more likely to stay home and never venture forth in the darkness. This will contribute greatly to your biking safety.

Another negative light to my mind is the heavy bulbous sort you mount permanently on your handlebars. These run on batteries and give you the disadvantages of both weight and clumsiness.

The only light I can give a hearty endorsement to is the Wonder Headlight, which costs only about $5 and runs on a 4.5-volt battery. It is bright, adjustable, and normally is visible from 500 feet. It has its own plastic handlebar mounting rack and can be put on and removed quickly. The light can be lifted out of the rack and used as a flashlight. Since it's small (5 inches x 2½ inches x 1¼ inches and only 9 ounces), you can always take it with you and avoid ever tempting the fates and the felons.

I've long wondered why someone doesn't come up with something like a miner's helmet and lamp combination for night cycling. That way, when you turned your head, the light would shine on what you wanted to see. Also, if you should meet with a night-time accident, the skull, that site of the most serious cycling injuries, would be protected.

THE ODIOUS ODOMETER: We all like to know how far we've ridden. It gives a great feeling of accomplishment, not to mention an amount of ego-speak material. ("Yep, I did 37 miles last Sunday before breakfast.")

How do you figure your miles? You can get in your car and measure them by driving the route, but this more than somewhat defeats one of the main purposes of bike riding—staying out of your car.

You can take the gear number you rode in (providing you rode in the same gear for the whole trip), count the RPM you cranked (providing you kept cranking at the same RPM for the whole trip), calculate the results on a cadence chart (see Appendix E) to get your miles per hour, then figure out how long you rode and multiply or divide as the case may be. This method has obvious problems of inaccuracy and time consumption and boredom.

There is a third possibility. You can get yourself an odometer. This is a small device you attach to the fork. You then attach a little pick to the spoke of the front wheel and every time the wheel turns, the pick moves the odometer wheel one click, registering the distance traveled. Lovely and simple and inexpensive, yes, but it has one slight drawback. It can drive you insane with its incessant twang, twang, twang. I had one on my bike and could only endure it for a week before I decided I was pedaling myself straight to the booby hatch. I removed it.

Reluctantly I must conclude that there is no really good way to calculate mileage. Perhaps it's all for the best. We human animals tend to subconsciously exaggerate our accomplishments, and without exact methods of mileage calculation our ego-speak stories can be even more satisfying. ("Yep, I did over 50 miles last Sunday before breakfast.")

BIKE CARRIERS: Unless you're giving up owning a car altogether—and my compliments to you for your strength of character—you're going to need some automotive way to tote your bicycle. This makes it possible to get to the traffic-free scenic spots where the cycling is pleasant going on delightful and sometimes even ecstatic.

If your car happens to be a station wagon or van, you're in luck. With a standard or intermediate wagon or van you can easily tuck away two bikes. Even with a compact wagon, all you have to do is remove the bike's front wheel and you're in business. The problem with two bikes in a wagon, though, is that one is semi-lying on top of the other, causing you to run the risk of damaging some of the more delicate components. It's helpful if you can get your clutches on one of those heavy quilted blankets the moving companies use. (On my last move, one of the alert uniformed moving men left one of these behind, bless him! Now I can pack two bikes into my wagon with minimal risk.)

If you have a car with a large trunk, you can probably squeeze in a bike, and maybe even two, if you remove the front, and maybe even the back wheel. The problems inherent in carrying your bike in a station wagon are compounded, though, by the tight squeeze factor of the usual auto trunk.

When you use your wagon or your trunk for bike hauling, especially in a compact, it's true that you've pretty much wiped out your luggage carrying space for long trips. And that brings us to bike carriers. These have the advantage of being able to carry your bike totally assembled. When you get to where you want to go, it's just a matter of liftoff and you're in biking orbit. The bikes don't lean on each other, either. Thus you eliminate the possibility of squashed and bent-up components.

A bumper-attached carrier has an added advantage. You can hang your bike on it at home and use it as a repair stand. I find it's very helpful to get the bike up off the ground so you can see what you're doing, crank the pedals when you're checking out the gears, etc. The method of turning a bike upside-down and resting it on its saddle and handlebars has never been effective for me except for tire changing, since when you're working on it, you have to remember that everything's backwards, and I have trouble enough remembering how everything works forwards.

If you do go for a bumper carrier in order to have this bike-repair-stand advantage, watch out for one thing. Be sure the tire of the bike doesn't ride directly over the exhaust pipe. If it does, the heat directly over the exhaust will heat up your tire and the explosion you hear will not be your car backfiring. If the exhaust is a threat, you can get an exhaust extender at almost any auto supply store.

Another beware that applies to any kind of carrier is this: make mighty sure your quick-release hubs are on good and tight. Once when I was hauling my bike I forgot to do this, and when I made a sharp turn, through the rear-view mirror I saw my front wheel rolling off on its own trip in the opposite direction from mine. Of course, you always also make sure your bike is securely attached to the rack. Those stretch cords I was touting work well for this, too.

If you decide on a carrier, which one shall it be?

That's almost as difficult to figure out as it is to decide what bike to buy. There are, in fact, just about as many bike carriers on the market as there are bikes, and they're proliferating like fruit flies. What you have to do to sort out what you want and need in the way of a carrier is to follow the Socratic method in a dialogue with yourself and ask yourself a few questions:

1. What kind of car do I have? Not all carriers fit all cars, and it would be a waste to spend time picking out a perfect carrier and then find it's one you can't use unless you spend time and money picking out another car. Even if the carrier's manufacturer claims it's able to fit anything on four wheels from a Honda Civic to a Rolls-Royce, be sure you get return privileges from the bike shop, just in case your car proves to be the exception to their universal fit rule.

2. How many bikes do I need to carry? Carriers range from those designed for loners to a foursome. I have seen some that take five or six, but those were do-it-yourself custom jobs. Be sure to get the kind of carrier you'll use most of the time—not for a once-a-year big group ride.

3. Where do I want to carry the bikes—roof, trunk, or bumper? Generally if you want to carry four bikes, this decision is made for you. It will most likely have to be a roof rack, although Allen makes a four-bike carrier that fits on the trunk of standard cars and over the back window of vans and wagons. If you want to use your carrier as a repair stand, you'll have to get

the bumper variety, and right now nobody makes a bumper rack for four bikes, but who knows what tomorrow may bring?

4. Will I be carrying a bike with a woman's or a mixte frame? If so, make sure that the carrier holds it securely. Some carriers are designed strictly with a standard frame in mind and while you may be able to put a bike with another frame on it, the bike may be held too loosely for the sake of safety and peace of mind.

5. Do I want a carrier that can also be used for other purposes? If you're a skier, there are some carriers, e.g., the Allen and the Curry, that can be converted to a ski rack. AMF makes a combination luggage rack and bike carrier.

6. Do I want to permanently attach the carrier or do I want to put it on and take if off as needed? If you decide on the permanent attachment, make sure you can get into your trunk or van or wagon door with it on. In fact, I'd make sure of that, even if I just used a temporary installation. My carrier, I feel, combines the best of both worlds. There's a permanent installation on the bumper that's a kind of three-sided box. The two upright arms of the carrier fold down when it's not in use, making the rack practically disappear into the bumper. It is so unobvious that it would take a very well-informed thief to spot it. (They steal racks, too!) I keep the crossbar, the carrying hooks and the stabilizing strap in the car at all times. Then, whenever I need to carry a bike, I can reassemble

the carrier in about three minutes. I'm ready to go
and so is my bike. I will admit that my rack's flaw is
that it's not the sturdiest and most stable one on the
market, but then the sad truth is no one rack is perfect.

When you've asked and answered these questions,
you're ready to lay siege to your bike shop with
something like, "Hello, there. I'd like a bumper carrier that will still let me open the trunk. I'd want it to
fit a '74 Toyota sedan. I want to be able to carry two
bikes, one of which has a woman's frame, and I'd like
to be able to convert it to a ski rack." ("Would you
mind repeating that, please?")

Style on Wheels

Remember the old saying about handkerchiefs—
one for show and one for blow? Bicycle clothing has
a similar breakdown. Some of the special cycling attire is as much for appearance as anything else (you
can make that statement about what's worn in almost
any sport), but some of it has a definite and important
utilitarian value, even though to the casual observer
it may appear that you're just dressing the part of a
cyclist.

It's certainly true that you can bicycle in anything
from a bikini to a business suit, and people do. After
all, when you're using your bike as transportation,
you'll probably want to wear the clothing that's appropriate to what you're transporting yourself to do.

If, however, your biking is the end in itself, you'll want to make yourself as comfortable as possible and therefore will want to dress in a way that's appropriate to that activity. To see just what is appropriate and comfortable, we'll start in on the ground and work our way up.

SHOES: The great basic truth about the shoes you wear for cycling is that they should fit perfectly. Rubbing makes blisters faster in biking than in walking. The pinching of a too tight shoe can cause incapacitating foot cramps.

The kind of shoes you wear will depend to a great extent on what kind of cycling you're doing. If you're going on a long tour, riding with toe clips, and don't intend to get off your bike for more than a few minutes for basic refueling and waste disposal, then special cycling shoes are definitely for blow rather than for show. They are made of lightweight leather. This gives you non-heaviness down there where it counts, and since it's moving, it counts even more. These shoes usually have cleats on them to keep your foot in the correct position on the pedal. Wearing shoes like these will keep you ankling along with optimum ease and efficiency.

On the other hand, if, although you plan to click off a goodly number of miles and are wearing toe clips to improve efficiency, you intend to get off your bike and stroll around, do a little sightseeing, maybe eat lunch in a restaurant, then you'll be better off not wearing cycling shoes. However, you should wear leather lace-on shoes of some kind for the obvious reason that they work better in toe clips than tennis shoes with their cloth tops. Leather's other advantage is a greater stiffness of the sole.

Now we come to a creature near and dear to my heart, the casual cyclist. This is the one who generally rides under 20 miles a day and in the course of an outing spends almost as much time off his bike poking around in the handiwork of nature and among the artifacts of civilization as he does on his bike pedaling. For this kind of bifurcated biking, tennis shoes are great. Their rubber bottoms cling well to the rattraps. I've cycled in leather-soled shoes without toe clips, and my feet slid off the pedals as if they were greased. Tennis shoes are also very comfortable for strolling around. The over-$20 investment in a pair of the top-quality leather or suede-topped tennis shoes, such as those made by Adidas or Tiger, is not profligacy. These outlast two or three cheap pairs and they give your feet—including your arch—support far beyond the poor powers of the low-cost limp varieties. (Double meaning of *limp* intended.)

SOCKS: Like the Palm Beach fashion of not wearing socks with formal attire, there are certain cyclists who prefer to ride sockless. They maintain that this keeps the feet from sweating as much and also tends to prevent foot cramps. Some cyclists also believe that the weight of a pair of socks makes a difference in their speed. (Probably it does, just about as much difference as drilling two holes in your chainwheel.) Obviously, the significance of socklessness would be apparent only to a cyclist of the toe clip and over 20-mile persuasion. The rest of us would feel more comfortable with the conventional cloth buffer between foot and shoe. Natural fibers such as cotton and wool are preferable to the synthetics that tend to store sweat next to the skin.

In cool weather I like knee socks when I ride with shorts.

PANTS: For freedom of movement you can't beat cycling in shorts. Even for a casual cyclist the constant tugging of the pants leg can be tiring. In all but really cold weather knee socks and shorts, especially if both are wool, can keep you warm enough most of the time. When they don't, you can keep the knees from freezing up in the early mornings and late afternoons by pulling on leg warmers.

Knee socks and shorts have the additional advantage of looking spiffy, and that's not to be entirely discounted. We cyclists have our vanities just like everybody else.

Cycling shorts are the pro cyclist's choice, but I don't think they're just for show for less serious types. They're made for comfort. There are no seams that chafe you and the chamois insert in the crotch gives just the right amount of softness and padding between you and the saddle. Since they're knit, cycling shorts move easily with your body. Even their color—basic black—is an advantage, because bicycle grease and chain muck do not show on them. There's a broad price range in cycling shorts ($10-$20), and it's wise to shop around. When you do, keep an eye out for quality as well as price. The more expensive wool jersey ones have warmth and breathability advantages. For a good buy in cycling shorts order them from Jeanne L. Crone, 1852 South Second St., Allentown, Pa. 18103 (215-797-5484). Hers are custom-made to your measurements for around $10, single thickness; $13, double thickness, 100 percent wool black jersey. Jeanne also makes arm warmers (around $5), leg warmers (around $7), and long tights (around $20).

You can convert regular shorts to semi-legitimate biking shorts by sewing in the chamois inserts yourself. You can buy pre-cut chamois in the fancier bike shops or if you have one pair of legitimate cycling shorts, you can use those as your model and cut your own.

If your chamois insert stiffens up with washing or cleaning, just squash and knead it with your hands (while you're not wearing the shorts, of course) until it softens up. I've seen the recommendation that you use salad oil for this softening process, but unless you wear lettuce underwear and perspire vinegar, this sounds like a poor idea.

If you don't want to go the leg warmer route on cold days, you can always use warm-up pants. In fact, warm-up suits or sweat suits or jogging suits or whatever name they go by in your parts are warm and comfortable.

I'm against blue jeans or Levis or denims (again select your regional appellation). The legs are too narrow, they are too stiff, especially when new, they're cold, and the inner seam is horrendously thick.

Despite the efficacy of shorts, most of us do part if not most of our riding in long pants. In this case, something to keep the pants legs from tangling up in the chain is a necessity. Even if you have a chain guard, you should still use something to keep your pants from flapping around and brushing the chain and other bike parts. They may not get tangled, but getting them greasy is not too pleasant either.

For a long time I rode with metal bicycle clips, but they seem to always be cut-off-the-circulation tight or so loose they drop down and dangle uselessly around your ankles. Far better are the cloth strips with Velcro on the ends. These can be attached to the exact degree of tightness you prefer and they stay that way all the while you ride. They also come in attractive colors and prints. Some have the added feature of being made of reflector material that gives you extra safety when riding at night. One brand of these is called Wrap-Around and sells for around $1.50 a pair.

SHIRTS: Unless you're a racer, I think the special racing or touring jersey is pretty much a show item.

Wearing one may cause you to suffer for your art, since, advertising brochures to the contrary ("wicks off sweat in warm weather"), they can get you hot as a son-of-a-gun. In really cold weather, even if you're wearing the wool rather than the acrylic variety, a cycling jersey won't be enough to keep you warm unless you're going 20 mph. You'll wind up having to cover up your flashy racing stripes and back pockets anyway. Besides, for the casual cyclist who's just moseying along, a racing/touring jersey seems a bit *de trop*—kind of like throwing in French words when English words will do just as well.

Any kind of soft, comfortable shirt will do. The really important consideration in cycling is comfort. This means both ease of movement and normal body temperature. As far as temperature is concerned, no one item of clothing is going to do the job even on a single day. The air temperature changes from morning to midday to evening and it changes as the wind picks up and dies down and it changes as the sun skitters in and out of clouds. You, yourself, also contribute to the temperature change as you pedal fast or slow, uphill or downhill, or as you stop and rest.

Most of the time on a day trip you'll need at least three items to take on and off—a shirt, a sweater, and a windbreaker. Sometimes you'll need all three. Sometimes the shirt and the sweater will be the best selection. Sometimes the shirt and the windbreaker are the more effective combination. Sometimes you can make it with the shirt alone. Sometimes you can take even that off. But you should have all these options. In that way you can always be comfortable, never dripping, never shivering, and you can use all your energy for pedaling instead of dissipating it in body temperature control.

In coldest winter you may want to add thermal underwear and substitute a parka for the windbreaker, giving yourself a few more layers to catch and hold heat.

Clothing comfort for cycling takes forethought, and that's the thought to keep foremost in mind.

GIFT FROM THE MOON: It would have been great if they'd taken the moon-shot money and cured cancer or worked out an alternate to fossil fuel, but since they didn't, we can at least utilize the peripheral products of the space program. One such development is a great little windbreaker. It's called the Apollo jacket. The fabric was developed for use in space suits—an aluminum skin bonded to nylon. This jacket is available from Norm Thompson (1805 N.W. Thurman; Portland, Or. 97209). There must be other sources for it, but I haven't run across any yet.

The Apollo jacket is ideal for cycling for many reasons. It folds into a tidy pouch, which you can stow in whatever size bike bag you have or, since the pouch has loops, you can wear it on your belt. It is lightweight, always a plus for weight-conscious cyclists. Because of its reversible feature, it's good both for cool-going-on-warm and cool-going-on-cold weather. When you wear the silver (aluminum) side out, it reflects the heat, and when you wear the navy side out, it absorbs the heat while the silver inner-side stores in your body heat.

For the topper, it has a hood built into the collar. Its only drawback is the around $35 price—and still ascending. But that's not too outrageous for what is, in effect, a $30 billion jacket.

GLOVES: Those fingerless cycling gloves, like cycling shorts, look as if they're for show, but really aren't. They help you grip both handlebars and brakes. The most valuable contribution cycling gloves make, though, is helping to prevent compression nerve damage in the hand. In the course of riding there's a tendency to squash the nerves in the hand between your bones and the handlebars. You can develop numbness and, in later stages, weakness in the fingers and hand. Good cycling gloves with chamois-padded palms can be a barrier between you and nerve damage.

When winter comes, those fingers hanging out in the cold can louse up your bike color scheme by turning blue, in which case you'd better slip on something more conventional. I like ski gloves, because they have the padding that prevents the above problem and they're also very warm. I once rode with wool mittens, but although your fingers can band together for warmth, you can't get much of a handle on the handlebars with them.

HAT: My favorite cool-to-cold-weather cycling hat is a navy watch cap. It's wool and therefore warm. It can be pulled down over the ears on really cold days, and it can be wadded into a small ball and stuffed into a corner of your bike so it's always handy when the weather turns round. The only drawback with a watch cap is that it makes the wearer, *any* wearer, look like Lennie in *Of Mice and Men*. You can get knit stocking caps that are a little more stylish. And if you want something in the vicinity of $8 that's chic and versatile, look for the Belgian wool five-way cap that some bike shops stock. This has a visor and is good for almost any temperature because the sides and back can be rolled up or down.

Another cold-weather help is a headband that goes around the ears. You can get these in all colors in ski shops. They're good both with and without hats.

In summer I like to ride with a tennis visor, because it keeps the sun out of my eyes and off my face, yet lets the top of my head breathe. If you prefer to cover the top of your head to avoid getting too much sun on your skull, there are a lot of cycling caps available at the bike shops. Unless you have a bizarre brand of bike, you may be able to get one with the emblem of your own bike. Rugged types who don't care about leathering up skin and acquiring squint lines often bike with a sweatband or nothing on their heads.

We'll discuss the pros and cons of helmets in the safety section.

RAIN IN THE FACE: When you bike in the rain, you have your choice of how you get wet. Will it be from above or below? Will it be from the outside in or the inside out?

If you wear a poncho, the water will bounce off the top of you but splash up from the street below. If you wear waterproof coveralls or a jumpsuit or leggings under a poncho, you will shed rain from the outside but collect an equal amount of wet in the form of sweat from within.

If you cycle along in your regular clothes, you'll get soaked from the outside in, but it will be nice fresh rainwater. A lot of people find this an exhilarating experience as long as they're not commuting to work at Merrill Lynch, Pierce, Fenner & Smith in a Brooks Brothers suit.

When you come right down to it, the only satisfactory thing to wear in the rain is a roof over your head. Not only is it impossible to keep dry any other way, but biking in the rain is the most unsafe activity you can pursue short of skydiving without a parachute. If potential death is no deterrent, the fact that it's hellishly hard on your bike, especially the bearings, may be.

chapter 8

BIKE MAINTENANCE FOR PEOPLE WHO WOULD RATHER BE OUT RIDING

There are five good reasons to do the minor maintenance and repairs on your bike yourself:

1. It saves time. If there's a little something wrong with your bike or a little something that needs to be done to keep it operating at the optimum level, you can frequently take care of it yourself in a jiffy. Dragging it into the shop, getting the situation analyzed, leaving it to have the work done, and returning to pick it up can take days or sometimes weeks in the get-ready-for-summer or back-to-school rushes.

2. It can save you a lot of money. Although the price of parts is ascending like everything else, labor is the big cost in any repair job.

3. It will make it possible for you to handle breakdowns on the road. Even if spending time and money doesn't bother you, being stranded in the middle of nowhere with a flat or a chain that keeps slipping off the sprocket will.

4. You may find you enjoy working on your bike. It may give you tactile kicks like bread- or pottery-making. It may give you feelings of capability that the complex modern technological world seems intent on driving out of you. If this turns out to be the case, you can progress to major repairs and complete overhauls and multiply the advantages mentioned above by ten. You may even become such a bike repair junkie that you start doing it for your friends and thereby earn money or goodwill, both of which are scarce commodities these days.

5. Even if you find you detest messing around with bike repairs, doing a few of the basic ones will benefit you. Ever after when you take your bike into the shop for maintenance and repair you will be so glad someone else is doing the dirty job that you'll never ever whine about what it costs.

THE MAJOR AND THE MINOR: How do we draw the line between major and minor repairs? That's simple. If I can do it with ease, it's minor. I guarantee that if I can do it, you can do it. I promise I will not ask you here to do anything I haven't done. In fact, I won't ask you to do a few things I have done, such as greasing bearings, because I found them taking more time than they're worth to someone who doesn't get his jollies from messing with machinery. Here, then, are the maintenance and repairs any bike owner should learn to do for himself.

If you do have an overwhelming desire and the concomitant mechanical ability to delve into major overhauls and repairs, there are a good number of detailed repair manuals to lead you through the intricacies and not mislead you too drastically. I've listed some of these in Appendix B.

Putting Air in Tires

This isn't as easy as it sounds, because there are a few variables to take into consideration. If you've invested in the high pressure pump with the built-in gauge already recommended, your tire-filling problems at home are solved. You may, however, have a need sometime when you're out riding. I've already mentioned the fact that the pump you carry on your bicycle is not designed for bringing your tires up to full pressure; so if you repair a flat on the road or find you have not enough pressure in your tires for some other reason, you'll want to head for the nearest gas station to bring them up to the right level. Here danger lurks, so much so that some experienced cyclists maintain that you should never under any circumstances fill your tires at a gas station.

If you're a woman, and a woman who's a cut above middle in looks and a cut below middle in age and on top of it you're wearing biking shorts, you may have trouble keeping the alert uniformed attendant from galumphing up and venting his gallantry by filling your tires for you. Unless he's an expert at filling 10-speed bike tires (and it's eight to five he won't be) then there's an eight to five chance he's going to blow the tires right off the rims. It's unbelievable how little air it takes at a gas station to fill a 10-speed bike tire. Whatever your gender, you must know how to fend off the attendant and do it yourself.

When you *do* do it yourself, always do it with short little shots, pft-pft-pft-pft, feeling the tire in between each pft. If you give it one long pfffffffft, that sound is likely to terminate with a great ka-POW, followed by a string of oaths that goes with the realization of how much time flat-fixing is going to take or how long the walk home is going to be.

Gas stations usually have gauges on their pumps to check the pressure, but I find I'm so concerned with not getting too much air in and with getting the head off the valve in a hurry that I have trouble reading the gauge and I prefer to operate by feel. After having pumped the tires up so much at home, where exact pressure is so easy to attain, and having squeezed the tires many a hundred times to see how they feel when they're at the correct pressure, I find in a station that I can pft and squeeze until I hit them just about on the air button.

Incidentally, the pressure that's marked on the side of the tire is not a hard rule. Since I weigh only between 100 and 105, I don't need quite as much air as it says to support me. A person heavier than average may need a little more to keep the tires from flattening out under his weight. Also, since I usually ride in the desert, if I fill my tires in the morning in the summer, I underinflate them slightly to allow for expansion later in the heat of the day.

This may seem like a lot of carrying-on over a minor point, but since tires are your only contact with the planet as you pedal, keeping the pressure at the right level is vital for comfort, safety, and wear and tear.

Quick-releasing Your Hubs

Those levers you flip for easy removal of front and rear wheels are a great convenience, and I recommend them. But they have their problems. Lots of women don't have strong enough fingers to squeeze them firmly closed, and lots of men don't give them the attention they deserve. Believe me, they deserve attention. The annals of cycling horror are replete with tales of wheels falling off. Note: The rule is if a wheel is going to fall off, it always does it when it will do the most damage—in heavy traffic, in the middle of a fast downhill run, when there's a pack of cyclists hard on your tail—or all three.

In order to avoid a fast, wheel-less trip to the hospital, it's important to understand exactly how quick-release hubs work. Releasing the levers is easy. You turn them away from the wheel to their full open position and the wheels become loose in the drop-

Tightening the quick-release lever

outs and drop out. Putting the wheels back on again and getting them really tight is the tricky part. You reinsert the wheel in the drop-outs with the lever closed but the nut on the right pretty well loosened. Then you open the lever and you tighten the nut. You try to close the lever. You'll have to either tighten or loosen the nut until the lever is almost-but-not-quite impossible to push closed. Sometimes it's easier to open the lever fully and twist it rather than the nut, but, of course, in this case you have to hold the nut secure while you rotate the lever.

There are several snags in this supposedly simple procedure. First, you don't have enough hands to center the wheel between the brake pads, hold or turn the nut, and keep flipping the lever. Then there's the problem that on the less expensive quick releases the nut is only knurled and you can't turn it as far as you need to with your fingers; you need pliers. (Campy's and Shimano's best releases have little loops to hold onto.) And then there's the major problem of not being able to press the lever hard enough to close it in a really tight position. Try using the heel of your hand, bracing your fingers against the fork or the flange. There's nothing too wrong, either, with lightly hammering it closed with the rubber heel of your shoe.

As always, the rear wheel has a few additional snares because of the derailleur and also because we amateurs don't know just how far to push the wheel into the drop-outs. (They're not like the front ones where you simply go all the way.) What you do is pull the wheel all the way back on the derailleur side. Then you straighten the axle in the frame. (Campy's rear drop-outs have a little stop screw that takes care of all this for you.)

How should you set the levers? Both on the left

and pointing backward so that they can't catch on anything and get knocked loose.

Flat Tire Changing and Tube Patching

To change a tire and patch the tube you need a set of bike tire irons (cost around $1) and a patching kit (cost around 50¢), both of which can be purchased in any but the most understocked of bike shops.

Tire changing is the one kind of repair I prefer to do with the bike turned upside-down, resting on the handlebars and seat, rather than hanging up on some kind of repair rack. It's easier to remove and replace wheels this way. Anyway, flats have a habit of occurring when you're out on the road where repair stands aren't necessarily at hand.

The first and most obvious step is to remove the offending wheel from the bike. When it's the front wheel, this is a cinch, especially if you have quick-release hubs. If you don't, just remove the nut with a wrench. (You may have to hold the nut on the other side of the wheel with another wrench.)

When it's the back wheel, you first have to remove the chain from the freewheel sprocket. To do this you'll need to push the derailleur body back to release the tension on the chain and give you room to work in. Try to remember before you begin to shift gears so that the chain is on the smallest sprocket of both the freewheel and the chainwheel. If you forget to do this, though, the world is not lost. When you're ready to replace the wheel, just push both shifters all the way forward and then put the chain on the smallest sprocket on both the freewheel and the chainwheel.

When you've got the wheel off, lay it on the ground or on a workbench. Remove the valve cap and let out any vestige of air that remains in the tube. You can usually get the air out by poking the valve with the reverse end of the valve cap. If that doesn't work, press the little pin in the middle with a screwdriver.

Take one of the three tire irons and hold it so the bend with the notch in it is away from you. Insert the rounded flat end between the tire and the rim. When you insert it, make sure the end with the notch in it is pointing to the sky rather than to the ground.

Now gently and carefully, so as not to tear the bead, pry the lip of the tire out and over the rim. Attach the notch of the tire iron to the spoke and *hold it there*. It's supposed to hold itself there. That's the whole principle of the notch. I find it flips loose as often as not, though, and that flip can propel it with unseemly force toward eye, nose, and tooth.

By the time you've got the second iron in place, you've probably loosened things up enough so you can insert the third iron and slide it along, releasing the tire from the rim. Just pull out the first two irons you put in. Once the tire's really beginning to let go, you don't need the irons between tire and rim any longer. As soon as you can, stop using the tire iron and start working with your hands. (Hands are much less hard on the bead.)

When you've released one side of the tire from the rim, put the stem in the 6 o'clock position and pull all the tube out except the stem section. Then you

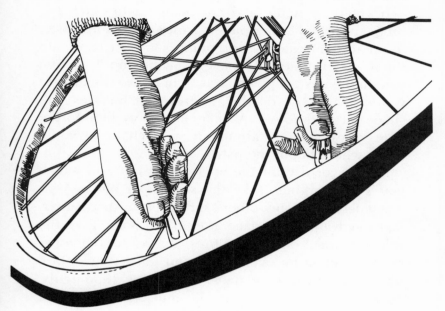

Prying off a clincher tire

should be able to get the tire off without using the irons again.

When you have the tire totally off the rim, take the tube out of the tire for patching. If you're working out on the road, of course, you'll have been clever enough to have brought along a spare tube or two, since one of the basic commodities for tube patching—a bucket or laundry tub of water to locate the hole—just may not be available. (A lake or other body of water could be used, but they aren't everywhere either.)

If you're at home and are planning to patch the tube (and you'd better plan to, since new tubes cost a lot more than patches do), pump some air back into the tube. You want it to make dramatic bubbles when you do the next step, which is to immerse the tube in water. When you do this, a stream of bubbles will shoot out of the hole. As soon as you've located the hole, draw a circle around it with chalk so you'll know where to put the patch.

Let dry or dry off the area of the tube on which you'll be working. Take the sandpaper out of your tire-patch kit (or any other sandpaper for that matter) and rough up the surface around the hole. Take the rubber cement out of your tire-patch kit (or any other rubber cement for that matter) and smear a layer of it on the roughed-up surface. Let it dry thoroughly. Take a patch from the tire kit and cut it to fit the roughed-up surface area. Thrift tip: You usually can get two or three patches out of one patch from the kit, because they're much larger than you need to cover the infinitesimal holes that tubes usually get. Thus can the person who's followed my advice and plunked down the many dollars required for a chrome molybdenum double-butted frame and all-alloy components save maybe a penny on tire patches.

Press the patch firmly into place. Pump just enough air into the tube to give it a bit of shape and make it easier to handle—but not enough to make it cumbersome. (If you're using a new tube, pump it most of the way up and then let air out to the bit-of-shape point. This gets rid of the wrinkles and folds that could get caught between the tire and the rim.)

Before you put the tube back into the tire, run your hand carefully around the inside of the tire to see if you can find and get rid of the thorn or bit of glass or whatever caused the flat. If you don't do this, you may get a duplicate flat with the first turn of the wheel. Also, check the rim to make sure the rubber strip that protects the tube from the spoke ends is in place. Sometimes this slips a little to the side, exposing the tube to the hazards of internal puncture.

If all seems to be in order, stick the valve of the tube through the hole in the rim, pulling it all the way out and then pushing it halfway in again. The bead may not seat if the stem is pulled tight. Fit in one side of the tire all around the rim by hand. Use a tire iron to pry on the last few inches if you have to.

With a tire iron, pry the tire onto the other side and slide the iron along, feeding the tire into the rim. Be careful when doing this prying and sliding that you neither pinch the tube with the iron nor catch the tube between the bead and the rim. Also try not to chew up your rims with the tire iron. This makes them look crummy and marks you as a sloppy worker. It doesn't help the bike's resale value either.

When you've pried and slud (as Dizzy Dean used to put it) your tire back onto the rim, tug the valve all the way out again, pump the tire to full pressure, put the wheel back onto the bike, making sure to center it in your brakes if you don't have the quick-release kind, and ride off.

General Lubrication

Bikes require both grease and oil on a regular basis—just like cars. Grease is thick; oil is thin. Greasing is not for amateurs, but oiling is. I'm against getting yourself into the grease job, because it requires special tools and know-how. You have to get to the bearings by opening up the hubs, pedals, bottom bracket, and headset. Since greasing of bearings has to be done only about once a year, why not leave it to an expert? If you put over 100 miles a week on your bike, however, or you ride a lot in the rain or through water, your bearings will need grease more often. (Whenever you get water into your bearings, look out.)

As for oiling all the exposed moving parts, anybody can do that—and should. Buy a good bicycle oil or, better yet, use WD-40. Attach the little red plastic pipe to the squirting hole so that you can direct a small amount to exactly where you want it.

And where do you want it? On the front derailleur pivot bolts (1); rear derailleur jockey and tension rollers and pivot bolts (2); brake lever pivot bolts (3);

freewheel (4). Besides all this, brake and gear cables have to be lubricated wherever they enter or exit the plastic housing. This lubrication job should be done

Points to oil regularly

about once a month. If you're an enthusiastic tourer, more often.

Clean and Lubricate Chain

When you transform a dirty, gritty, clogged mess of a chain into a clean, glistening, well-lubricated one, there's such a difference in how a bike rides that you suddenly feel jet-powered. Since the condition of the chain makes such a difference in the quality of the ride and since chain-cleaning and lubricating is so much easier to do than it would appear, it is a minor tragedy that ninety-nine out of a hundred cyclists never touch their chains between overhauls and consequently ride around with a chain that looks like a rope of chewed-on licorice—and rides about like one, too. If you ride your bike regularly, say around a hundred miles a week, you should clean and relubricate your chain every month. But unless you're not riding your bike at all, under no circumstances should you let it go without care for longer than three months.

You will need to buy for this minor operation a chain-link remover, which costs only around $3 and can be bought in any bike shop. Sorry, folks, but you simply cannot really clean a chain without taking it off the bike, and this means opening a link. If you want to cheat occasionally, though, you can try using Schwinn's Spray Bike Degreaser or Petrochem's Chain and Derailleur Klean.

Before you take your chain off, look long and hard and carefully at how the chain is threaded through the back derailleur. Here's an illustration of how a Shimano derailleur is threaded, but there are slight variations for each brand. Also notice which sprocket the chain is on in both the back and the front, because you'll want to return the chain to the sprocket it was on. If you forget to do this, though, you can handle the situation in the same way you handled it when you removed the rear tire to fix a flat and forgot which sprocket the chain was on.

Lay the chain across the rivet remover so the two prongs extend up through the chain and the rivet is positioned in a direct line with the bit. Twist the handle of the rivet remover until the bit pushes the

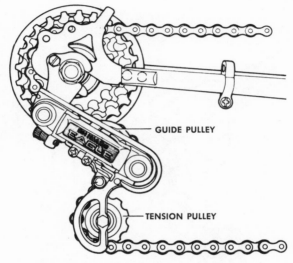

GUIDE PULLEY

TENSION PULLEY

Threading a Shimano rear derailleur

rivet almost, but not quite, out the back. The first few times you do this you'll have to keep taking the chain out and checking to see how far along the rivet is. Later on you'll be able to tell when you've pushed the rivet far enough by seeing how far it extends from the back. You want the links to be able to separate but you want the rivet still clinging to the back edge, because that makes it easier to put the chain back together again.

If you should push the rivet all the way out, you can get it back on by putting the two links back together and slipping the extra bit that comes with

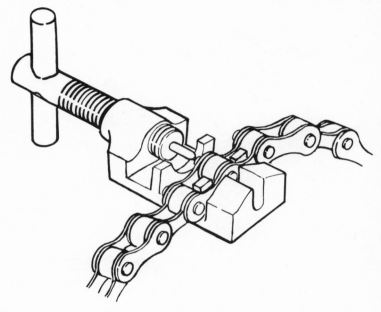

Removing rivet of chain link

the rivet remover through the holes the rivet goes into. Lay the chain in the rivet remover in the opposite direction, placing the knocked-out rivet between the outside edge of the hole and the bit of the rivet remover. Twist until the rivet is just barely into the outside edge of one link but doesn't join it with the other. Pull out the extra bit, remove the still separated links, and proceed.

After the links are separated, slip the chain off. Put the chain in some metal container that's big enough so you can lay the whole thing on the bottom. I use an old fruit cake tin. Pour in enough solvent or paint thinner or kerosene to cover the chain. (Stay away from gasoline; it's far too dangerous.)

(An entertaining aside: Bike shop personnel love to ding bike books, often, I have to admit, with reason. One shop owner claimed that all bike books copy each other. Each one perpetuates the mistakes of those that came before and adds a few new ones of its own. His favorite example was an American author who must have been copying, among others, a British bike book. This writer advised that a good inexpensive substance to clean your chain with is paraffin. The bike shop owner gave a chuckling shudder at the innocents who might be gluing up their dirty chains by pouring hot melted wax over them, not realizing, as the author apparently didn't, that in Britain paraffin is the name they use for kerosene.)

While your chain is soaking in whatever you use to clean it, put some of the solvent in a small can, take a toothbrush and a rag and clean the grease and dirt off the teeth of the sprockets of both the chainwheel and the freewheel, as well as the sprockets in the derailleur. Don't slosh the solvent around carelessly. Just clean and wipe what you're supposed to clean. There are a number of bike components, parts, and attachments that don't take kindly to the likes of paint thinner and kerosene.

If you have the time, let your chain soak overnight. If you want to get the chain job over with and the bike back on the road, work over the chain with the toothbrush until it's clean. Stretch the chain out on a newspaper to dry. Again, if you're in a hurry, pat it dry with a rag or paper towel.

Rethread the chain through the derailleur and the freewheel and chainwheel sprockets from whence it came. Be sure to have the separated links meet in the middle of where the chain stretches straight across from freewheel to chainwheel. It's easier to work on that way.

In order to rejoin the chain, you will need to relax the tension on it by pushing the derailleur tension wheel forward. (It helps if you have someone do this for you the first time, because when you're unsure of what you're doing, you need your hands free to work on the rejoining of the chain.)

Fit the links together and place them in the rivet remover *reversed*—or in the reversed rivet remover. It helps to slip the extra bit that comes with the rivet remover through the holes in the two links to keep them joined while you're attempting to put the rivet back in. As you twist the rivet remover to push the rivet in place, the extra bit is pushed out. Be sure you get the rivet in exactly as it was before so that the ends extend equally from each side. If you twist it too far through, just reverse the rivet remover and push the rivet back a little.

When the chain is rejoined, take it out of the rivet remover and grasp it on each side of the newly joined links and wiggle it back and forth to see if it's too tight. If it is (it's not uncommon for this to happen), try to loosen it by wiggling it some more. If that doesn't work, take a thin-bladed screwdriver and stick it between the edges of the links where they meet and gently pry them apart a little. Wiggle some more. Gently pry and wiggle until the link is as flexible as all the other links.

Now you're ready to oil the chain. The best substance to use is a motorcycle chain lubricant like Lubriplate or Chain Life. These motorcycle chain oils, as far as I'm concerned, are the only good things to come out of the motorcycle subculture. (And I do mean sub.) I particularly like Chain Life by Petrochem because it cleans as it lubricates and it repels sand, dirt, mud, and grass. This keeps it from getting gucked-up as rapidly as some of the other lubricants. It's nonsticky and clean-looking itself. If you get it on your person, you don't look as if you've been working in chimneys.

Test out your bike with its clean, newly lubricated chain and enjoy the experience of feeling you have wings on your wheels.

Brake Adjustment

The do-it-yourself brake adjustments include tightening the cables as they stretch, realigning the arms when they get askew, and realigning and replacing the shoes when they get lopsided or worn. Brake adjustments differ somewhat according to brands and according to whether you have the side-pull or centerpull design.

CABLE TENSION: When you grip your levers as hard as you can, if there's less than 1 inch clearance be-tween them and the handlebars, it's time to take up the cable slack. When the slack is not too great, you can take it up easily with the adjusting barrel. (Not all brakes have these, but check carefully; they're in different positions on sidepulls and centerpulls.) Loosen the lock ring screw and unscrew the adjust-ing screw until you've tightened the cable enough. Then retighten the lock ring screw.

If the adjusting barrel turns all the way out and the cable's still not taut enough, then your job is a little more complex. You've got to loosen the cable anchor bolt and pull more cable through. This takes some tools—a small wrench, a pair of pliers, and a friend's hand. (If you don't have a friend, there's a tool called a third hand you can get.)

Have your friend hold the brake shoes tight against the rim of the wheel. (I hope your friend has a good steady strong grip.) Loosen the anchor bolt, pull a little cable through, retighten the bolt and see how your brakes work. If you've pulled too much cable through, the brakes won't release from the rims. (It's as though you had a permanent friend's hand on them.) So it's back to the anchor bolt to undo a little

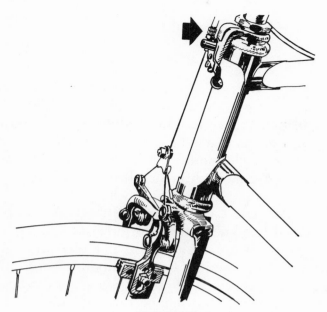

CENTERPULLS

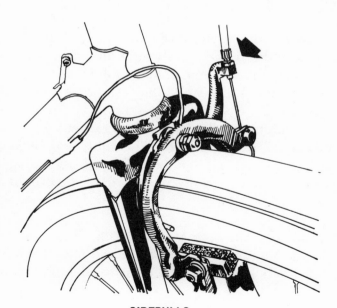

SIDEPULLS

Brake adjusting barrels

of what you've done. The shoes should remain about ⅛ inch from the rims on both sides.

Don't forget that there are two brakes to adjust— the front *and* the rear. The rear is often a little harder to get to, so tackle the front first, then you'll be experienced for the more difficult job.

REALIGNING THE CALIPERS: Often the brake calipers or arms will get knocked to one side or the other and you have to center them again. For this problem I recommend a procedure frowned upon by most bike-repair experts. But I've found it works, and when it comes to making adjustments, I'm a pragmatist. Just take a heavy screwdriver, place it against the spring behind the arms, and tap it lightly with a hammer. Tap a bit, check; tap a bit, check; etc., until you have the arms centered again. Be sure the bolt holding the brakes to the frame is still tight after this maneuver. (This may have been your problem all along—the bolt wasn't tight and the whole brake simply twisted.)

One thing you don't do is try to bend one of the brake arms back into place. The alloy most brakes are made of is not a bendable material and what will happen is that it will live up to its name—it will break.

REALIGNING OR REPLACING SHOES: There are four brake shoes, two on the rear brake and two on the front. Each shoe consists of a metal holder with a rubber block inside. The holder is attached to the brake arm with a bolt and nut (sometimes this is a special bolt called an eyebolt). To adjust the way the shoe lines up against the rim you loosen the nut and fiddle a lot.

When brake levers are pressed, shoes should hit the rim fully *without* touching the tires and without hanging below the rim. As I mentioned before, they should be about ⅛ inch away from the rim when the levers are released, but you may have to go for up to ¼ inch to get a good alignment.

Sometimes the problem is that the shoes toe in at the front. This is okay, but they definitely should not toe in at the back. If they do, this usually means the shoe is bent and it's best to replace it.

When shoes get worn down, you can buy new rubber to slip into the metal holder or you can buy a whole new shoe. (Take one with you to match it perfectly. There are lots of different brands of shoes with slightly different dimensions.) Before you start the job, press your brake quick-release button, if you have one. If not, you might want to remove the wheel, because it's sometimes awkward to replace pads with the wheel in the way.

If replacing the rubber only, pry out the old and slip in the new so that the closed end of the metal holder is at the front. Otherwise, the rubber will simply shoot out the first time you apply the brakes.

Incidentally, new shoes may not seem to fit perfectly. They may want to stand away from the rim more at the bottom than at the top. Don't fret too much about this. They'll fit properly after they've been broken in. Some rubber shoes even come already tapered so that they're perfectly aligned without a breaking-in period.

Derailleur Adjustment

Derailleurs are simple mechanisms to those who're familiar with them, but they look terribly confusing the first time you pick up a screwdriver and cast a nonmechanic's eye in their direction. If you bought your bicycle new, you may be lucky enough to have received an owner's manual. This is a real boon, because there are more than sixty different derailleur models on the market and each one has its own design particulars and peculiarities (though the principles in all are generally the same). The only help I can give you here is to point out the most common adjustments you'll want to master and indicate how they're handled for most brands.

You may try to talk yourself into believing you can get around ever having to tamper with any part of the derailleur system—and this includes the gear levers, the wire cable from the levers to the front and rear derailleurs, and the derailleurs themselves. I wish I could give you such assurances, but I can't. Everything about derailleurs is precise and is hanging right out there in the open vulnerable to battering, bending, and weathering. Every time your bike falls over on the derailleur side or you bang into something with that side, there is a strong possibility that you'll have to readjust whatever you knocked out of whack. But be not distressed. The manufacturers thought of all this, and they've given you nuts and screws to make derailleur precision-tuning easy.

I find it easiest when working on derailleurs to put the bike up on a repair stand of some kind. As I mentioned before, certain bumper carriers can double as a repair stand. Putting the bike up on a stand makes it easier to see what you're working on and also makes it possible to crank the pedals and shift into different gears.

THE GEARSHIFT LEVERS: The gearshift levers have a little nut at their base. Many of these are in the form of rings so that you can loosen or tighten them with your fingers. There is a purpose to this. Often for good reason—or for no good reason—the levers become loose. When they do, the result is that the derailleur keeps slipping out of the gear you put it in and shifting you into a different gear entirely on its own. When this happens, tighten the ring (or wing nut, or plain nut). But be careful not to tighten it too much or you won't be able to shift gears at all.

THE FRONT DERAILLEUR: The main idea here is to keep the adjustment screws set so that when you shift, the chain goes onto the chainwheel you've selected and not beyond it. What the screws do is limit the motion of the cage. In other words, they're stop screws.

The low gear (inside chainwheel) screw is usually on your left as you sit on the bike; the high gear (outside chainwheel) screw is usually on the right.

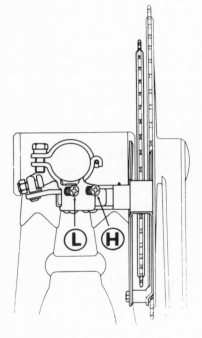

Front derailleur adjustment

(There are exceptions to this depending on brand, and some changers have only one screw.)

If your chain insists on moving too far to the left and slips over and off when you shift onto the inside chainwheel, tighten the low-gear screw (left one). If the derailleur carries the chain too far to the right and off when you shift onto the large chainwheel, then tighten the high-gear screw (right one).

It's possible for the adjustment screws to become too tight, in which case undershifting is your problem (the derailleur doesn't move the chain far enough to get it onto the chainwheel sprocket you've selected). To correct this, loosen the offending screw.

THE REAR DERAILLEUR: The rear derailleur, like the front one, has a high and low adjustment screw to keep the mechanism from overshifting or undershifting. The screw closest to the ground is usually the one that adjusts for the high gear (smallest sprocket). If the chain wants to ride off the smallest sprocket, you tighten the high-gear screw.

Now let's turn to the largest sprocket. Here the problem concerns the chain moving too far toward the other side of the bike frame and hanging up in the spokes. If your chain rides beyond the biggest sprocket and hangs up in this way, you tighten the low-gear screw.

If the trouble is that the chain won't move far enough to get into the highest or lowest gear, loosen the appropriate screw.

A way to check to see if you've adjusted the derailleur correctly is to shift the chain onto the smallest sprocket, stand behind the bike and sight the derailleur jockey and the smallest freewheel sprocket to see that they're lined up and that the chain runs straight up and down between the two. Do the same with the largest sprocket.

If you get the adjustments made correctly for the highest and lowest freewheel sprockets, the three in the middle should be correctly adjusted automatically. If there's some difficulty with the alignment of

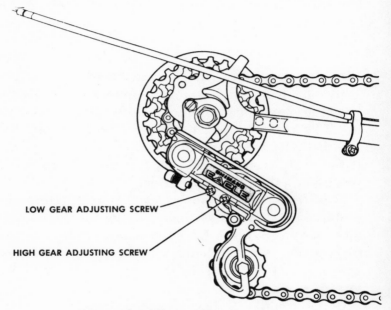

LOW GEAR ADJUSTING SCREW

HIGH GEAR ADJUSTING SCREW

Rear derailleur adjustment

the middle sprockets when you shift into the middle gears, then the fault, dear Brutus, is not in our derailleur adjustment but in our shifting technique.

Tightening Nuts and Bolts

Nuts and bolts that ride and rattle along on bicycles constantly work themselves loose. This means

that you have to periodically check them for tightness, unless you want to run the risk of having the
seat or the brakes or the gear give you a nasty sur-
prise at some moment when you're depending on
them to serve you well. So get out that trusty screwdriver and crescent wrench and methodically go over
all the screws and nuts and bolts, checking them for
tightness. Often you'll find nothing at all loose week
after week. Then one day you'll find a nut upon
which your hide depends suddenly finger-working
loose, and as you tighten it up again, you'll conjure
up in your mind's eye the different disasters that nut
could have caused you and you'll be immensely re-
lieved that your imaginings cannot now be converted
into reality.

By the way, new bikes often have loose parts
thanks to careless or inattentive assembly. (It can
happen in the best of shops, although it's less likely
than in the worst of shops.) Always check out your
new bike yourself before you ride it.

ENOUGH IS ENOUGH: When Mae West said, "Too
much of a good thing can be wonderful," she wasn't
talking about bike maintenance and repair. Too much
of *that,* especially when it's done by amateurs, can
be rotten.

What is too much? In my opinion, too much includes just about all the rest of maintenance and repair. I've already pointed out the hazards of greasing
bearings. Another *verboten,* as far as I'm concerned,
is truing wheels. Never has anything looked so easy

and yet been so fraught with disaster traps. My bike mechanic, Larry Branson, told me that after one of the popular you-too-can-be-the-compleat-handyman magazines covered wheel truing in their regular bicycle column, a parade of very false wheels rolled into his shop. Some of these were so totally ruined that they had to be replaced.

This brings us to a large beware. Beware of magazine articles that tell you how really simple it is to do all manner of complex bike repairs. Beware even of bike-repair manuals that purport to tell you how to do everything there is in the realm of bike repair and maintenance.

In an interview with the Los Angeles *Times,* Eugene Sloane candidly admitted that when he wrote the second edition of his *Complete Book of Bicycling,* he threw out 80 percent of the material in the first edition, because it was inaccurate or out of date. "If you tried to spoke a wheel from my first book, you'd go out of your mind," he said.

A letter he received from a reader of the first edition said, "Dear Mr. Sloane: Thanks to your book I have taken my rear wheel apart and now I can't get it back together."

Even if you're a mechanical marvel, the advanced stages of bike repair aren't all that easy. Listen to Sam Braxton of Braxton's Bike Shop in Missoula, Montana: "It takes a trained craftsman using infinite care to do proper adjusting and work on the 10-speed."

The last time I was in Gus Dandos' shop in Van Nuys, California, I started talking with another customer, who happened to be a Porsche mechanic. I asked him if he did all his own work on his bike. "No," he said, "I don't. A bike is something special. It's more complex than it looks. I've been thinking about doing my own work for about a year now. I'm still just thinking about it, though."

My advice to you is to do the same—just think about it.

chapter 9

CAUTIONARY NOTES

WE HAVE MET THE ENEMY AND HE IS CARS: The following is an item printed in its entirety from the classified section of the Victor Valley *Daily Press:*

> FOR SALE
> 10-speed bicycle with generator light, also hospital bed complete with side rails and trapeze.

Doesn't need much comment, does it? But I won't let that stop me from commenting anyway. Bicycles and accidents go together like love and marriage.

As for bicycle accident statistics, I have some bad news and some bad news and some more bad news and hardly any good news at all. The federal Consumer Product Safety Commission ranks bicycles as America's number one product hazard. In 1973 over

400,000 people received hospital emergency room treatment for bicycle injuries. (And like rape, far from all are reported.) In the same year 1150 riders were killed. Interestingly enough, only 5 percent of the injuries came from a bike being involved with an automobile, but those were the serious ones. They caused 90 percent of the deaths.

WHO DONE IT? Who got involved in most of the accidents? A California study showed that in 60 percent of the bike-car accidents the rider was in the five-to-fourteen age category. But adult cyclists are far from paragons of pedaling safety. In fact, the number of older persons killed riding bikes has been rising so dramatically that in 1974 one-half the death victims were adults.

Since I have more contact with grownups than with children, most of the bicycle horribles I've heard about lately are in this rapidly increasing grownup division. In the last six months alone at the college where I work two professors have been knocked off their bikes while riding to campus. One escaped with only bruises and scratches and loss of dignity, but the other got a broken pelvis out of the encounter. Also during this brief period of time the son of another of the professors was killed on his bike and since the son was in his early twenties, he too qualifies for the adult category. Now if I in my limited circle of acquaintances know of this many cycling accidents involving adults in this short period, I don't feel we can read the statistics and be at all complacent.

NOSTRA CULPA: In bike-auto accidents, who is most often at fault, rider or driver? You probably didn't guess right. Although we're always ranting about motorists, it's most often the bicyclists; 78 percent of the time, in fact. What we cyclo-sinners have done to bring about disaster is usually one of the following:

We have come onto a road or street and ridden into the path of an oncoming car.

We have drifted in front of a car in the middle of the block.

We have jumped the gun on a stop signal or just plain run through one without stopping at all.

We have ridden at night without a light.

We have ridden on the wrong side of the road.

We have ridden a bike that had a structural or mechanical defect. This is estimated by the Consumer Product Safety Commission to be the cause of 17 percent of the bike accidents. That's why they're always wrestling with mandatory safety standards for bicycles. To get a free fact sheet from them, write to Bicycle Safety, Consumer Products Safety Commission, Washington, D.C. 20207.

We have not yielded the right of way.

We have been riding too fast for road conditions.

We have made a turn from the wrong lane. That is to say, we didn't turn from the lane that was closest to the direction we were turning.

We have ridden in the middle of the street.

What to do? Obviously we should go and sin no more. In fact, according to the National Safety Council, four out of five motor vehicle–bike injuries could be prevented if we never disobeyed a traffic regulation. Obviously you should contact your department of motor vehicles to find out what those regulations are in your state.

Other safety precautions include:

1. Watch for heads through the windows of parked cars ahead of you. A head usually has a hand somewhere in its vicinity and that hand may well be reaching toward the door handle in order to open the door in your path and cause you to dump yourself.

2. When crossing at an intersection that is obviously hazardous because of a traffic flow as fast and heavy as the blood from your ears will be if you get hit, turn yourself into an instant pedestrian. The moment you get off your bike and onto your feet you are accorded all the rights and privileges and protections of a pedestrian. These are a lot more than those of a cyclist, including as they do going into crosswalks and having the auto traffic screech to a halt in deference to you (at least, in California).

3. When you signal for a turn (obeying the traffic regulation), be sure you do it well before you make your turn, not while you're making it. Turning without both hands on the handlebars is an invitation to an accident. (Accidents are very eager to accept any invitations offered to them.)

4. Be particularly cautious in dealing with rain and ice and snow-slick streets. Extend your caution to not riding on them at all, if you can possibly avoid it. By the way, slightly wet streets are even more hazardous than thoroughly rain-washed ones, because a little water combines with the residue of oil and road muck to make the surface as slippery as oiled BBs on glass.

5. Another time to exercise caution is when you see drainage grates in your path with the grill arranged to catch bike wheels. A wheel caught in one of those can be the end of the ride. In fact, if your community has a lot of these grates—or even a few—it's worth a letter of protest and suggestion for improvement.

6. Always ride single file. One bicycle width is enough or more than enough to fill up any available cycling space on a street or road. But don't nullify this caution by tailgating the bicycle ahead.

7. Yield to all pedestrians. As cars are to bicycles, bicycles are to pedestrians. Let's behave the better toward pedestrians than cars behave toward us. This isn't just for the pedestrians' safety. Knocking a pedestrian over frequently results in knocking yourself over as well.

8. Don't ride under the influence of anything from alcohol to Valium. You need all the faculties you can muster when biking in traffic. And you *can* get arrested for drunk riding. The motor vehicle code on this applies equally to bikes and cars.

Even when you throw all the safety rules into your personal skull computer and always act on them, you still can't be certain you'll be safe. You have to ride defensively and be on the *qui vive.*

BIKEWAYS AND MEANS: Now finally we come to one safety solution that you'd think every cyclist could agree on—the creation of special bikeways or marked routes for bicycle riding. Here is safety *par excellence.* Or is it? Not according to many members of the bicycle establishment. Before we get into the controversy, first let's see what bikeways are.

Although different states number the classes of bikeways differently, most are beginning to agree on the basic three, Class I (bike paths), Class II (bike lanes), and Class III (bike routes).

Class I—Bike Paths

These are specially constructed and are totally separate from streets or roads. They are for the exclusive use of cyclists. Examples of these are paths through the state forest on Martha's Vineyard and the 72-mile aqueduct ride in California. Some college campuses have also created bike paths.

Bicycle life would be beautiful if the nation were gridded with a network of Class I paths leading to everywhere you might ever want to go. Even in our wildest hallucinations, however, we can't imagine this ever happening. The cost per mile of an exclusive 8-foot-wide asphalted Class I bikeway with good

terrain and without signals is—brace yourself—
$75,000 per mile. As a result there are so few Class I
bikeways and they're so located that they're pretty
much restricted to recreational rides.

Class II—Bike Lanes

These share the road with automobiles. They are a
lane marked for bicycle use by a painted stripe
(usually) or a raised concrete border (hardly ever).
They give only limited protection from automobiles.
It is even more limited when cars are allowed to park
in these lanes.

Critics of Class II lanes claim they don't cut down
at all on accidents. Most accidents occur at intersec-
tions, where lanes becomes totally confusing to both
drivers and riders. For example, when a cyclist wants
to make a left turn, does he leave the bike lane and
go to the left traffic lane for his turn or does he cross
the street on the right and pick up the new lane on
the other side? And how about the car trying to turn
right? Does he do it from the second lane from the
curb or does he invade the bicycle lane? How about
cars coming out of driveways?

Class III—Bike Routes

These bikeways are not really worthy of consideration; indeed, they are beneath contempt. They are
also a snare and a delusion and a fraud and a phony
and a sop and tokenism at its most flagrant.

Class III bikeways are merely a series of signs

placed along a street declaring it to be a bike route. Supposedly the purpose of these signs is to "alert drivers to the fact that cyclists may be using this route." Baloney and other less palatable substances! The only real purpose of these is to allow local politicians to pose for pictures dedicating the routes and to allow the community to declare—and show on maps—that in the true and vigorous spirit of encouraging cycling they have created x number of miles of bike routes.

In my opinion and that of a number of other clear-thinking, reasonable, and generally fine folk, these Class III bikeways should be rubbed out to keep bicyclists who try to ride on them from being the same. Since those worthless bike route signs cost taxpayers $50 a copy, the money would be much better spent on something of genuine value to bicycling.

A SHOULDER TO LEAN ON: The California State Department of Transportation has another good idea, a kind of alternate to bikeways. They encourage the "provision of well-maintained shoulders along as many roads as possible" for cyclists' use. When I rode on the very busy four-lane highway from Palm Desert to Indio, I feared no evil, because the shoulder was wide and flat and clean and all mine. I don't think this shoulder had been specifically designed with cyclists in mind—there were no lines or signs to that effect—but it might well have been, so effective was it as a bike route.

Incidentally, some roads have an edge stripe, which is a continuous line running along the right to separate the traffic lane from the shoulder. While these haven't been put there for cycling pleasure and safety, they do a good job with both. Edge stripes tend to keep cars in their place and presumably us in ours when we're riding the shoulder.

THE CONS OF THE PROS: Bikeways, shoulders, paths, lanes, routes, call them what you will, most of the cycling establishment is dead set against them for one logical reason. They fear that where special routes exist cyclists will be restricted to them by law and that their rights of the road will be jeopardized.

I think these fears may be unfounded. Witness the position taken by the California State Department of Transportation in their *Highway Design Manual:*

> The fact that standards have been established for designating portions of some roadways as bike routes is not intended to affect a cyclist's right to other roads as well . . . the opportunity for a cyclist to ride his bicycle to virtually any destination he may choose should be preserved, restored, or initially provided, as the case may be.

This should make everyone happy, except, of course, the motorist, who is bound to feel threatened and hostile and unwilling to allow others in his formerly exclusive domain.

Personally, I've ridden on all classes of bikeways

and, though I detest Class III ones, I love Class I's and Class II's. In Palo Alto around the Stanford campus I tested out the Class II system and felt much safer riding there. I felt that for once instead of being an irritating interloper in an alien and hostile lane, I had a place to call my own. When I found myself on streets without lanes, I felt threatened again. It's amazing the difference a stripe of paint makes.

HELMETS: Harold Wooster of the Potomac Pedalers Touring Club pithily remarks, "There are two sorts of bicycle riders—smart ones and stupid ones. The smart ones buy bicycle helmets *before* they fall on their heads; the stupid ones wait until they've wiped out before they start thinking about helmets—if, in fact, repeated concussions leave them anything left to think with."

Wooster makes an excellent point here, a point that's backed up by all the bike shop men I've talked to. The majority of their helmet sales are to people who have been injured in a bike accident. If you're going to be one of the smart ones and buy your helmet before the fact of the disaster, which helmet is best? The consensus is that there is no perfect helmet.

The racer's helmets—those puffy strips of leather that crisscross your skull—are sometimes referred to as "leather hair nets." This gives an indication of at least some people's opinion of how much protection they offer. I knew a fellow who got a concussion while wearing one. This may sound as if the helmet failed him, but the examining doctors agreed that he would have been dead if he had been wearing no helmet at all.

Some cyclists favor hockey helmets, others mountain climbing helmets and still others claim polo helmets are the answer. Motorcycle helmets, which admittedly offer the best protection, are almost universally rejected because of their weight and the way they cut down on peripheral vision.

There are an increasing number of helmets specifically designed for bicycle riders. Mountain Safety Research (P.O. Box 696; Tacoma, Wash. 98401) has come up with one that shows a decided family resemblance to those they designed for mountain climbers. If I had to recommend one helmet above the others, MSR's would be it.

Really, though, the only practical solution for most of us is to shop around and try on all the various kinds of helmets available. Choose the one that's most comfortable and that you feel the least foolish wearing. In other words, find one you can live with and are most likely to wear. Buy it. A less perfect helmet on the head is safer than a near perfect helmet at home in the closet.

Incidentally, even if you persist in remaining negative on helmets, you may eventually be forced into a more positive attitude. Many bike clubs are now starting to require helmets on their rides. I also suspect that in these days of burgeoning bicycle safety laws, we may see helmets written into law before too long.

SAFETY FLAGS: Safety flags are the small triangular pennants—usually in a fluorescent material—attached to the rear of the bike by means of a long metal, fiberglass or wooden pole. In their favor it can be said that they serve to make a low-profile, low-visibility vehicle a lot easier to spot. In traffic the flag sticks up above even the cars. Out on the road if you're descending a hill, a driver coming up behind you can spot your flag and know that something's ahead to beware of.

In their disfavor are their minor accident potentials. The metal and fiberglass poles can catch on things and snap back and flail the bicyclist like a whip. The wooden variety can catch on things and splinter, leaving a hazardous jagged remainder. Then, too, should you have to make an emergency rearward exit from the bike, it's possible to tangle yourself up in the pole as you try to leave. The final problem is not one of safety but effectiveness. The flags have a tendency to wrap themselves around the pole so they can hardly be seen.

THE LAST MILE IN SAFETY MEASURES: Bikeways, helmets, safety flags and regulations of the Consumer Product Safety Commission aren't going to be able to do the ultimate job of keeping cyclists alive and pedaling. It's going to take something more. It's going to take three measures—brace yourself for a shock—that cyclists who appeared before the National Highway Traffic Safety Committee were *practically unanimous* in agreeing were the three best ways to increase biking safety.

1. Education of the cyclist by qualified instructors. This education should include on-the-road practice in traffic conditions.
2. Rules of the road to be followed by all cyclists, regardless of age, in all situations including on and around bike routes.
3. Enforcement of these rules with appropriate penalties to cut down on the violations that are the main cause of collisions between bikes and cars.

If a miracle of the magnitude of getting all cyclists to agree on something is possible, then anything is, maybe even safe bicycling.

Dog Coda

Cyclists are hounded by dogs. A dog doesn't even have to be vicious to cause trouble. Some of my most unpleasant experiences have been with friendly dogs. I remember one Irish setter in particular. I took to calling him Irish Rover, because I would run into him in distantly separated parts of the desert. Literally run into him. With a wide grin and a lolling tongue and a wagging tail he would amiably crisscross the road in front of my bike, making me constantly slam on my brakes lest I go down in a tangled heap of chrome and bone.

Even worse, though, are the strange and hostile-seeming dogs who approach you at full bark with bared fang. What are you to do? Almost everyone agrees that pedaling swiftly away from the hounding hound is the very best tactic. In order to be able to do this, it helps if you're on the downhill or at least the flat. (I remember once on a slight uphill incline I was outraced by a savage Pekinese.) It also helps if you're a fairly strong and fast cyclist, although dog-activated adrenalin can fire up the most languid among us.

Another technique is to pedal along at your normal rate and ignore the sound and the fury. Many times the dog just feels compelled to defend his territory and if you let him get the obligatory barks out of his system, he'll trot back to his front yard content at having done his dogly duty.

You can also yell, but make it loud and simple and staccato and a familiar negative like "No!" or "Bad!" A friend of mine always yells something obscure to a dog vocabulary like "Get back in your yard, you mutt." She's never been bitten yet, but dogs don't back off immediately at her oblique comment.

One of my favorite methods of repelling dogs is to give them a squirt in the face from my water bottle. The bottle has a hole in the head and when I squeeze, it directs a thick stream of water into what I'm aiming toward. I've caught many a dog full in the face. Most of them looked shocked and backed off. One memorable dog, however, drank it down like *vino tinto* shot out of a *bota* and continued his pursuit. I did slow him down enough to get away, though.

There is an aerosal product called Halt with which you are to zap dogs in the face. A bike shop attendant told me it was made with cayenne pepper, but he may have been funning me. I can only presume that this product works, because I am too chicken to try it. I have the abiding fear that in a moment of stress when the fierce brute is charging me, I might accidentally point it in the wrong direction and zap myself full in the face.

Another dog-dispatching item which, like the water bottle, has the advantage of always being on the bike anyway, is the tire pump. Many of the more physical cyclists advocate unhitching the pump and giving the offending canine a smart whap across the nose.

The reasons I don't consider this too smart are two. First, you have to take one hand off the handlebars and twist around, which can make balance precarious. (That's true of the water bottle squirt method as well.) Second, in order to do the whap number you have to be within fang distance of the dog and, cunning instinctive creature that he is, it's very possible that he's going to get you before you get him.

The Bicycle Thief

THE RAPE OF THE LOCK: No method of bike locking-up is infallible. Case-hardened chains have had good press, because it's mighty nigh impossible to cut through them. But I heard from a friend who always kept his Motobecane case-hardened-chained-up that a thief still managed to get away with the bike. How? He poured Freon on the chain to make it cold and brittle. Then he whapped with a cold chisel and snapped it easily in two. This is one of the reasons the flexible cables are now considered superior to chains.

There is also a newly developed locking system called the Lockalarm. When a thief tries to cut its cable, it sounds off like the giant's harp in Jack and the Beanstalk and can be heard for half a mile away. This gives you double protection, but then you do have to carry its weight with you at all times and you do have to pay around $20 for it.

The very best locking system I've seen was a swarm of bees that settled on a chainwheel, but it's hard to find those, even in the most completely stocked of bike shops.

Naturally, it's not always the entire bike that goes. The parts and accessories being valuable, too, sometimes they go when the frame remains. Anything that can be removed easily is unfair game. Wheels with quick release hubs are a popular item, and that's why, when you chain your bike, you need a chain long enough to wind through the wheels as well as the frame. Many canny cyclists remove the front wheel and chain it together with the back wheel and frame.

ANTI-RIP-OFF RULES:

1. Lock your bike. Lock it always. Police recover an amazing number of expensive bikes that have their locks and cables wrapped around the seat post. Lock your bike even when you're just leaving it alone for a few minutes.

2. Register your bike with whatever licensing and registering system your community has available. If you don't, the police have nothing to go on when they're trying to recover it for you. Also, if you don't register your bike or at least make note of its serial number, you have no real means of proving it's yours. If the bike is recovered by the police you may have trouble extracting it from them. That's understandable. The police can't just have people dropping in and saying, "Hey, that red Italvega over there is mine," or they'd just become a free bike distribution service.

In case you don't know it, the serial number is usually engraved under the bottom bracket. The Peugeot has it on a little metal plate down there. According to the police aide I saw checking for stolen bikes on the University of California's Santa Barbara campus, this feature makes Peugeots the thieves' favorite. The identifying plate can just be pried off. If you have a Peugeot, you should engrave the number on the bottom bracket.

3. Go to the police station yourself to check through the recovered bikes. If you just report your loss by telephone and wait for its return, you may

wait in vain. I've heard of people who have given the police the total description, including the serial number, and who, after waiting several weeks for word that it had been found, have gone down to the station and found their bike sitting there. The police say that so many bikes are now being stolen and recovered that it's impossible for them to check them all against the stolen bike records.

There is a movement afoot to start a nationwide system of bike registration and computerized recovery, but until this is done, we're on our own.

4. Work for (and nag for) safe bike parking areas. Employers and merchants should provide places where bikes can be kept without risk.

INSURING SUCCESS: As for insurance, I'm not sure it's worth it. See page 218 for the premium schedule for one such policy. This particular one is a $25 deductible, unless the bike is a total loss.

You could also check with your own insurance company to see if your bike can be written onto one of your existing policies.

Personally, from my admittedly limited experience I have become an insurance cynic. In most policies the small print always seems to take away what the large print gives. I usually find that the things that happen to me and my property just happen to be the things that aren't covered. Still, if you're interested in investigating bicycling insurance further, you might write to the outfit that calls itself "the bicycle folks," Devonshire Coverage Corporation, P.O. Box 76983 B, Los Angeles, Ca. 90076.

Premium Schedule

BICYCLE VALUE *	PREMIUM
0—$100	$12
$101—$125	$14
$126—$150	$16
$151—$175	$18
$176—$200	$20
$201—$225	$22
$226—$250	$24
$251—$275	$26
$276—$300	$28

For bicycles valued in excess of $300 add $2.00 per $25.00

* Includes new retail price plus accessories and sales tax.

chapter 10

BIKE MOSEYING,
THE ADULT RECREATION

What exactly is a mosey? Well, one person's mosey is another person's grueling speed tour and still another's plodding crawl. A mosey is what you want it to be and what you make it.

Maybe my idea of a mosey will give you something to start with so you can create your own mosey pattern. My moseys can be in the town or country. They can be all day, half a day, or even an hour or two. Although the distance covered is usually under 20 miles, the speed varies. Sometimes I travel at a good clip; sometimes I ride in more of a meander. The important thing is that whatever speed I'm going I don't feel rushed. I'm not in a hurry to get somewhere, because I'm already there. I'm on my bike and enjoying all the sensations of air and sun and moving muscle. Or maybe I'm off my bike viewing a view or prowling a shop or art gallery or museum or eating a picnic lunch or perhaps lunching in a little U.S. counterpart of a bistro or trattoria (or, let's be realistic, a hamburger stand). No matter what, I'm packing in the joys of biking and exploring and existing.

I may be alone or with friends. When I'm alone I don't feel lonely, and when I'm with someone else I don't feel crowded or constrained.

And that is bike moseying to me.

BIKE PACK PACKING: For a pleasant mosey besides clothing extras (caps, gloves, rain gear, sweater, etcetera) you need to pack several basics in your *boîte* or bag, plus a few personal options.

Basics: One or two spare tubes (or if you're a sew-up freak, one or two spare tires). This is necessary even if you're going on a short mosey. A flat even a mile or two from home can leave you with an unpleasant bike-pushing walk if you can't fix it on the spot.

A tool kit containing tire irons, a crescent wrench, pliers, and a screwdriver. If you're the fastidious kind, you might want to throw in an old pair of cotton gloves to work in. Should you get your hands greased up doing some kind of repair, the grease on your hands will be quickly transmitted to your bike and your clothes.

A mini first-aid kit. This should contain a tube of

antiseptic cream, a few Band-Aids of various sizes and one large bandage to be on the safe side. A roll of tape is handy, too, since it can do double duty for bike and human repair. For preventive maintenance you might want a chap stick and a tube of suntan cream or, if you're highly susceptible to sunburn, a sun screen.

An extra sandow or two, in case you want to bind something onto your bike rack—the irresistible purchase in a shop you pass and may not pass again, or a spectacularly attractive piece of driftwood, or who knows what until you find it.

A pocketknife. Particularly good are the Swiss Army knives, because you can get them with just about anything on them you might need, including scissors, a screwdriver, and a corkscrew. Speaking of the corkscrew, I consider that an essential, if you're a wine and cheese picnicker (isn't everyone?). A knife-corkscrew combination I like is the kind waiters carry around in their pockets. It's the flat, leverage style, with the fold-out knife for cutting the lead foil. You can use the knife for bread and cheese and salami cutting, too. Some of these also have a bottle opener on the end.

A thin sheet of plastic. This should be big enough for two to sit on comfortably. You may meet a friend. This is invaluable for preventing damp pantseats when you stop for lunch or a rest break. Large plastic trash bags can be used for this purpose, too.

Money. This always useful commodity is an essential on a bike trip. Be sure you have the proper change for making phone calls—several phone calls. You never know what or how many emergencies will come up. Carrying a credit card isn't a bad idea either.

A small package of tissues. One's nose tends to outrun the bicycle in the wind.

A map. It's very handy—sometimes vital—to have along a map of the area you're biking in. This is true even if you're biking in your own home town. Local maps can usually be obtained from the Auto Club or the Chamber of Commerce or real estate offices.

Sunglasses. These are almost as imperative to keep miscellaneous debris from blowing into your eyes as for protection from the sun's glare. According to an oculist I talked with, the gray tones offer the best protection and visibility.

A small notebook and ball point pen. You may want to take or leave notes. You may want to give your address or phone number to a compatible someone you meet. There are all kinds of possibilities with a notebook and pen.

Optionals: A camera and film. Don't drag these along unless you're really a picture taker and really intend to use them. I've seen people carry their cameras everywhere and never take them out of the cases. All this does is add extra weight and probably cause you to ruin film from leaving it in a bag in the hot sun.

Cosmetic needs. Don't go into this in any great depth. If you're too fussy about your appearance, it spoils your fun. A few Wash 'n Dries can get rid of the surface road grit and make you minimally presentable if you go into a restaurant or shop.

YOU CAN TAKE IT WITH YOU (but it ain't easy): To help you plan far-away moseys, I was thinking of providing you with a breakdown of the bike-carrying policies of the bus companies, Amtrak, and the airlines. I decided to leave it out, though, as this is a nonfiction book. What the transportation companies *say* they can do and what actually happens often are worlds apart. Indeed, the on-the-line personnel sometimes act as if they don't know what a bicycle is, let alone how to ship it. I've come to the conclusion that those who do the actual ticketing and luggage handling never see the beautiful copy put out by their advertising department. Another more charitable possibility is that policies are so constantly being changed ("always striving to serve you better, et cetera, et cetera") that what you read or heard happens to your bike no longer holds true or else doesn't hold true yet.

My advice then is this. Contact the local office of the airline or bus or train and ask them what their current policy is. Try to get the name of the person who states this policy so that if someone tries to hassle you as you're attempting to hand over your bike, you can say, "But your Mr. Blank assured me that a bicycle could go as one of the two allowable pieces of luggage," or "Your Ms. Whatchamacallit said there was a flat charge of $8 for a bicycle no matter how much it weighs." Do this same checking at your destination for your return trip. Policies differ drastically from one terminal to another. For example, the airline on which I flew to Boston took my bike free going and charged me $8 coming home.

IN THE BAG: The first time I took my bike flying, I really wanted to do it the right way. I went out to a fancy bike shop and bought a special canvas bag for bike carrying. It had inner side pockets for the wheels (which you removed) and a space for tools. The outside was emblazoned, "Fragile—Racing Bicycle—Please Handle with Care." That, I thought, should do it. It did. Since I had reduced my bicycle to a tidy package, the airline handled it the way they handle tidy packages. The bike bashed its way down the chute and onto the revolving luggage carousel. The bag might as well have had "destroy me" written on the side.

When I unzipped the bag I found the derailleur off. (I should have packed it in hand-carved styrofoam.) The fork tips and drop-outs were bent. (I should have begged or bought two axles to put between them. The blocks of wood I had taped in were knocked out.) But mainly I should have kept the bike looking more like a bike. I think they might have treated it a little less brutally if I had.

If the transportation you're taking permits it, just wheel the bike to the baggage room and hand it over.

That's the best. If the airline provides you with a carton or a plastic bag, use that. If they don't provide anything but still require the bike to be packaged, try to get a box from a bike shop. Don't buy a bag like mine. The cost is exorbitant (around $50) and it provides virtually no protection. Another of its flaws (at least, of the one I bought) is that it doesn't work for a bike with touring handlebars. If for some mad reason you do invest in one of these bags, make sure it can accommodate your style of bike.

Should your bike be creamed by the luggage manglers, make a claim for whatever it costs you to get your bike put back together. They usually pay, not promptly, not cheerfully, but eventually and resignedly.

Hope for the future department: Larry Wuellner, Manager of Cycling Activities for the Auto Club of Missouri, envisions a "violin case on wheels" for transporting a bicycle on public conveyances. His organization has presented the idea to the bicycle industry. Let's hope they pick it up so that when our bikes arrive at their destination they won't be all out of tune and unstrung and we'll be able to make beautiful music with them.

IT ONLY HERTZ FOR A LITTLE WHILE: When it comes to car rentals for bicylists, *nobody* is trying harder. I wrote to every one of the major auto rental agencies asking if they now or ever contemplated renting "bikerized" cars. These would be like their "skierized" cars, except that instead of having a ski rack, they would have a bike rack. My answer from each was a resounding nope. They usually cited the lack of demand and the fact that the great majority of their rentals are to businessmen who would have no need of such an appendage.

Perhaps if all of us interested cyclists dropped the car rental agencies a line, they might take the hint. In the meantime all we can do is whine for a compact wagon or rent a car with a big enough trunk to carry the dismantled bikes in. The only other alternative I can think of is to bring along your own bike rack and attach it to the rental car. Since you're also bringing along your bike, that makes for an awful lot of bring-along, especially on an airline.

AUTO SUGGESTION: I differ with a lot of bicycle fanatics. I don't want every automobile off the streets. If I had to ride my bike to wherever I wanted to use it, I'd never get there, or if I did, I'd be too exhausted to do anything once I arrived.

Even if I fly or take a bus or train to the general area I intend to mosey in, I still need a rental car to get me to my final destination. With a car you have all the clothes and unguents and libations and reading matter and whatever other comforts a person of adult years—rightly or wrongly—tends to regard as necessities for an enjoyable holiday.

My goal in bike moseying is to park my car at the mosey epicenter and thereafter use only my bike or feet to get around. I daily bike out and back in a different direction. By the time I've left that area, I've ridden every ridable street and road. And every night after my twenty or so miles of biking and several more of walking, I've been able to take a bath and change into clean clothes and have a good dinner and sleep between sheets on a real bed.

I also do a certain amount of riding en route to my destination. If it takes a few days to get to where I plan to do my intensive moseying, I eliminate a lot of the literal pain in the rear end that a long-distance car ride is. Every morning I take a two-hour bike ride before I climb into the car and every evening I take another after I pile out.

THE RIGHT PLACE AT THE RIGHT TIME: Bike moseys are where you find them, and you can find them almost anywhere. You'll acquire an eye and a feel and a nose for them in short order. While you're developing your own personal detection system, I'd like to give you an idea of what I look for when I plan a major tour.

1. Scenic beauty. This is one of the greatest upliftings of a bike trip. For me, cycling through the warehouse areas and by junk yards and through the uglier neoned and billboarded urban sprawl sectors just doesn't do it. If the scenic area happens to have some kind of cultural or historical interest, that's the cherry on the cycling sundae.

2. Relatively flat terrain. It doesn't have to be as

flat as a dry lake bed, but as far as I'm concerned, honking hill climbs are not integral to my enjoyment of a bike mosey. Rolling terrain is fine, but with more steeps than that I grow reluctant. In general, I'd rather use my energy on horizontal, not vertical distance.

3. Good accommodations. The ideal hub of my bike mosey wheel has what I think of as a "maturity hostel," a comfortable hotel or motel or inn. It also has one or more good restaurants (the more the better, if I'm staying in the area several days). When I pedal home at night I want that home to be worth coming home to.

4. Benign weather. This means, as far as I can arrange it, having it cool but not cold, warm but not hot, and keeping those two cycling dreadfuls, the wind and the rain, out of my hair. Finding this kind of weather may take a little study ahead of time, checking with the chamber of commerce, et cetera, but it's worth the effort.

5. An absence of people. This is one of the hardest requirements to meet on this increasingly overcrowded earth, but it can be done. One thing that helps is to try to plan the trip when school is in session. Not only does this keep the kids themselves out of your territory, but carloads of vacationing families aren't out clotting up the roads either.

6. Good biking facilities. This doesn't mean a plethora of Class I or even Class II bikeways. Side roads and wide shoulders are just as good or better,

especially if you've been able to find point 5 above.

Now that I've set up these standards, I'll offer to you what I consider two ideal bike mosey places and times. I use these as my touchstones for perfection.

Ideal Mosey East—Cape Cod in October

Think of it as Holland in your own country. It's flat and it's surrounded by the ocean and, what with all the deep inlets and salt ponds and cranberry bogs, you feel that the land has been reclaimed from the sea. To complete the Dutch illusion, there are even several old windmills.

You can also think of Cape Cod as a flat Vermont. As a Southern Californian who never really gets to experience the change of seasons, I had been hungering and thirsting for fall foliage. My original plan had been, in fact, to bike Vermont and New Hampshire. Upon looking inside the New England bike tourbook a considerate Eastern friend had sent me, I changed my mind. Virtually ever route in those two states was marked "hilly" or "definitely hilly." Like Pierre Salinger, who refused when asked to participate in a Kennedy administration 50-mile hike, "I'm plucky, but not stupid."

As I changed my plan to Cape Cod, which the book described as "flat" or "rolling," I felt a twinge of regret over the lost leaves. It was an unnecessary emotion. The foliage of Massachusetts takes second place to none. In fact, there were more of my favorite blood-red leaves there than farther north.

Another reason besides the foliage for an October bike mosey on Cape Cod is that October is a seasonal shoulder period. The mobs and hordes and throngs of the Cape Cop summer have fled back to Harvard and the Chase Manhattan, but most of the hotels and restaurants haven't battened down for winter yet. Since business is way down, you have the dual advantages of off-season prices and a feeling that you have the whole glorious area as your private cyclodrome.

If you win on the meteorological lottery—and the odds are good that you will—you will have Indian summer, that most sought-after of seasons and the one that is perfection for bicycling.

For all its smallness (70 miles long) the Cape is actually fairly large for cyclists. You have plenty of choice. While it's hard to go wrong, it is best to avoid the more citified and trafficky parts such as Hyannis. This means you're better off on the Lower Cape, the part out toward the hook that starts at about Orleans and ends at Provincetown.

If you write to the Cape Cod Chamber of Commerce, Hyannis, Mass. 02601, they will send you a care package full of tourist information, accommodation directories, restaurant guides, boat schedules, in fact, everything you need to plan your own personalized tour. I can't resist, however, giving you my idea of five perfect bike-mosey hubs on the Cape itself and the two offshore islands, Nantucket and Martha's Vineyard.

SANDWICH: This gives you a total New England village flavor. In fact, from all appearances you could be in Vermont. There are lots of interesting things to do here besides biking in the green and rolling countryside. There's the Sandwich glass museum, the doll museum, and the unique 76-acre Heritage Plantation. A good place to stay is the modern yet traditional Daniel Webster Inn.

ORLEANS: Here a cyclist can find a home at the Governor Prence, where manager Joe Breen has a complete shop on the premises and will help you repair any minor and a few semi-major bike problems that may develop and keep you entertained with Cape Cod lore in the process. Biking around town and observing the classic Cape Cod architecture and checking out the beaches on both the ocean and bay side makes a fine day trip. Another is to pedal up to Eastham along the ample breakdown lane of the highway. Eastham is the gateway to the National Seashore and by the time you read this the bike route through it may be completed all the way to Provincetown.

PROVINCETOWN: This is called P-Town by the *cognoscenti,* of whom you'll find many in this cosmopolitan village out on the end point of the Cape. The best maturity hostel I can possibly imagine is Hargood House, which is made up of all different and all charming apartments right on the beach. They even have a distinctive bike-locking system that you might want to copy for your own home. P-Town has a bike route that takes you on a sand dune tour that auto drivers never see. Along with the great seafood you can find anywhere on the Cape, there are some excellent continental restaurants, including a Portuguese one called Cookie's. It features Portuguese dishes and wines the likes of which I've never tasted before and have always dreamed of since.

NANTUCKET: This is such a compact and manageable island that you can zap around it in one day, but it deserves to be savored for longer than that. Lovely empty roads and bike trails with wild grapes free for the munching. And all around the sea so blue it looks as if the indigo traders had a ship go down with full cargo. The town will cobblestone you to insensibility with its charm. The accommodations and restaurants are of the quality you'd expect in a place where the summer visitors are wealthy and discriminating and the permanent residents are no slouches either.

Leave your car in the dockside parking lot in Hyannis and wheel your bike on board the ferry ($1.50 for it each way). Boats for Natucket also leave from Woods Hole, but it's much closer from Hyannis.

MARTHA'S VINEYARD: This island is a big one and you'll need your car on it, if you mosey the way I do. The boat from Woods Hole has a large capacity for cars. Once there, hie yourself to Edgartown, the most charming sector and home of the homes of the old whaling captains. One of these has now been converted into the spacious and comfortable and tasteful Edgartown Inn. I don't know which I enjoyed more here, the room or the fantastic breakfast that included homemade cranberry bread.

Martha's Vineyard is loaded with bikeways. You can get a map of them at any stationery store or newsstand for $1.50. The routes are all graded. For example, the one from Vineyard Haven to Gayhead is "for grand tourismo champions and non-smokers only." The rest are all much, much easier.

Ideal Mosey West—Palm Desert in January

Yes, I said Palm *Desert*, not Palm *Springs*. Palm Desert's more famous neighbor is, to my mind, not for bicyclists, at least not for this bicylist. It's too crowded and too citified and the streets are too narrow to accommodate the traffic, let alone bicycles. But down the road a piece (13 miles), now that's another matter—wide uncongested streets and a marvelous feeling of wide-open Western space.

In January, Palm Desert is just winding up for its high season, which really starts rolling in February. Although the prices are already up, at least the crowds haven't arrived and you'll be able to find space in the motels as well as space on the roads. Another feature of January here is that there's something particularly engaging about biking around in your shorts in the warm sun in the classic month of unremitting frigidity.

Two moderately priced (for the area) places I've enjoyed are the Adobe and the Desert Patch. The latter is an especially homey place where the owners, Frank and Frances Messano, will carefully lock and cover up your bike from the nighttime desert damps and then, since it's right outside their bedroom window, keep an ear on it all night. The Desert Patch is also nice for grownups because it's an ageist establishment—no one under twenty-five is admitted. Along with swimming pools, most of the hotels in Palm Desert have hot water therapy pools to deknot your biking muscles at the end of the day.

If you should happen to be in the jet-set financial category, you could hang up your biking shorts at La Quinta, a spacious and elegant resort outside of town. It happens to be the only U.S. member of the prestigious French Relais de Campagne network.

As for biking terrain, it runs from gentle to flat. You can just ride off as far as the eye can see, and in the desert that's mighty far. There's a wide shoulder that takes you down to the desert date capital, Indio. On your way there be sure to stop in at Sniffs for a date ice cream cone or milk shake. You can also buy any number of exotic breeds of date there. They make perfect energy-restoring cycling snacks. I particularly like the bread dates both because they are supposed to be so nutritious as to be able to sustain life all by themselves and because they're very dry and don't glue themselves to each other when you carry them around in your bike bag. Sniffs also has a fascinating botanical garden to picnic in.

Biking around the Palm Desert–Indian Wells–Rancho Mirage area, you can enjoy heaps of man-made beauty in the form of the myriad of well-landscaped golf courses as well as the natural beauty of the desert which, once you acquire a taste for it, soon becomes an addiction. This part of the desert, incidentally, is so similar to Tunisia that Patton's troops trained here to get ready for North Africa.

The selection of restaurants is wide and varied and surprisingly inexpensive for such a posh resort. A special charmer for both the food and the atmosphere is the Nest in Indian Wells.

Things close down fairly early here at night. As a resident told me, "Everybody has to get up early the next day to make his golf starting time." This rhythm is good for the cyclist, too. He needs his sleep in order to get up early to make the sun's starting time. There's nothing more extravagantly beautiful than riding in a desert sunrise.

And here's the clincher for a Palm Desert bike mosey. Should perchance some careless motorist knock you off your bicycle, you need have no fear. You're there in the home of the Eisenhower Medical Center, where you can get the absolute best of medical attention and knit your bones in what looks more like the Hyatt Regency than a hospital.

National Park Moseys

You might want to try a tour through one of the national parks, both for the pleasure of it and as a preview of coming attractions. Some of the park service people have a dream, and it's one I share with them: no cars allowed in national parks.

Until that dream comes true, you can help the cause by taking your bike with you and using that exclusively for transportation once inside a national park. I did that in my favorite park, Yosemite, and it was perfect. Of course, Yosemite is very bike-oriented, anyway, with a bike loop through the valley floor and with well-organized and well-attended spring and fall bike rallies. (Write Marketing Department, Yosemite Park and Curry Co., Yosemite National Park, CA 95389 for information.)

Any national park experience is better for being on a bike rather than in a car. If enough of us show up there on bikes, we may start a trend even before the car ban becomes a law. For information on biking in national parks, contact National Park Service, U.S. Department of the Interior, Washington, D.C.

Miscellaneous Moseys

DECLARATION OF INDEPENDENCE: The Bikecentennial is a great breakthrough in independent bike moseying. In honor of our two hundredth anniversary the first transcontinental bicycle trail is being inaugurated. You don't have to bike the whole thing, of course. You can select such individual sections as the Kentucky Blue Grass Tour or the Colonial Virginia Bike Tour or where-you-will. There are services both for you and your bike along the way. There are also lots of group tours for those who want them and even some charter flights to get you home again. For all the details write: Bikecentennial, P.O. Box 1034, Missoula, Mont. 59801.

PACKAGE MOSEYS: There are organizations that have put together some dandy bike tours. Strangely enough, the most active of these is the Auto Club of Missouri. (What's an auto club like you doing in an activity like conducting bike tours?) They have tours available to every which where, including the likes of the chateau country of France and Nova Scotia and Guatemala and even Rio.

I love their bike touring philosophy, as expressed by Larry Wuellner. "Our Adventure Tours generally appeal to the individual who has several weeks of vacation, prefers traveling first class, enjoys the company of interesting individuals, appreciates art, architecture, historical sites, discussions with the denizens of out-of-the way places or has a particular fascination for natural phenomena ranging from birds to botany. Bicycling is usually just the best way of moving themselves through these experiences and not proof of a pioneer independence for them as it often is for the solitary sojourner. The Adventure Tours show the purpose is in being there more than getting there."

You don't have to be a Missourian nor yet even an auto owner to join these tours. For information, write to them at 3917 Lindell Blvd., St. Louis, Mo. 63108.

Another outstanding and active touring organization is the International Bicycle Touring Society (846 Prospect St., La Jolla, CA 92037). The "Huff-and-Puffers," as they call themselves, are led by the cycling surgeon, bon vivant and raconteur, Dr. Clifford L. Graves. They offer a wide variety of tours both in this country and abroad. Their approach is a mite more vigorous than the Auto Club of Missouri, but adult cyclists of all ages find happiness participating in these tours. Conviviality and high enthusiasm for cycling are more important requirements than extreme hardiness.

Another good group to join for tours is the League of American Wheelmen. For your membership fee of a mere $5 ($8 for a family) you get their bulletin, which is a good magazine full of cycling lore and lots of information on tours, short and long, undemanding and rigorous, domestic and foreign. Their address is League of American Wheelmen, Inc., 19 South Bothwell, Palatine, Ill. 60067.

Still another source of tour information is the classified section of the cycling magazines (see Appendix C). Some of the airlines are also getting into bike tours. Swissair vigorously so, American Airlines more tentatively. I suspect that if these begin to prove profitable, more airlines will become involved. Check with your travel agent and watch the ads in cycling and travel magazines.

APPENDICES

MAIL-ORDER SOURCES
OF BICYCLES AND FRAMES

Bike & Hike of Wisconsin, Inc. 7217 W. North Ave.,
Milwaukee, Wis. 53213.

Braxton Bike Shop. 2100 South Ave. W., Missoula, Mont.
59801

Cupertino Bike Shop. 10080 Randy Lane, Cupertino, CA
95014.

Pickering Cycles. 3454 North First Avenue, Tucson, Ariz.
85719.

Sink's Bicycle World. 816 South Washington Street, Marion,
Ind. 46952.

BICYCLE REPAIR MANUALS

Anybody's Bike Book by Tom Cuthbertson (Ten-Speed Press, 1971)

DeLong's Guide to Bicycles and Bicycling by Fred DeLong (Chilton Book Company, 1974)

Derailleur Bicycle Repair (Xyzyx Information Corporation, 1972)

The New Complete Book of Bicycling by Eugene A. Sloane (Simon and Schuster, 1974)

Richard's Bike Book by Richard Ballantine (Ballantine Books, 1972)

The Super Handyman's Big Bike Book by Al Carrell (Prentice-Hall, 1973) appendix C

CYCLING MAGAZINES

Bicycle Spokesman. 119 E. Palatine Road, Palatine, Ill. 60067.

Bicycling! 55 Mitchell Boulevard, San Rafael, CA 94903.

Bike World. Box 366, Mountain View, CA 94040.

Canadian Cyclist. Canadian Cycling Association, 333 River Road, Vanier, K1L 8B9, Ontario, Canada.

Cyclenews. 12 Cherry Street, Brattleboro, Vt. 05301.

High Gear. Box 2367, Stanford, CA 94305.

International Cycle Sport. Kennedy Brothers Ltd., Howden Rd., Silsden, Keighly, Yorkshire, England.

League of American Wheelmen Bulletin. 19 South Bothwell, Palatine, Ill. 60067.

Shimano World. 9259 San Fernando Road, Sun Valley, CA 01352.

appendix D

CADENCE CHART

GEAR RATIO	REVOLUTIONS PER MINUTE OF THE CRANK ARM										
	60	75	80	90	100	120	130	140	150	160	
30	5.37	6.7	7.5	8.05	8.95	10.7	11.6	12.5	13.4	14.3	MPH
32	5.71	7.5	7.65	8.6	9.55	11.45	12.04	13.35	14.3	15.25	MPH
34	6.0	7.65	8.15	9.1	10.15	12.15	13.2	14.2	15.25	16.2	MPH
36	6.4	8.0	8.5	9.65	10.75	12.53	13.95	15.0	16.1	17.2	MPH
38	6.8	8.5	9.06	10.2	11.4	13.6	14.7	15.85	17.0	18.2	MPH
40	7.15	8.95	9.55	10.7	11.95	14.3	15.5	16.7	17.8	19.1	MPH
42	7.50	9.40	10.0	11.25	12.55	15.0	16.30	17.5	18.7	20.1	MPH
44	7.85	9.85	10.5	11.8	13.15	15.7	17.0	18.3	19.6	21.0	MPH
46	8.21	10.3	11.0	12.32	13.72	16.4	17.8	19.2	20.5	22.0	MPH
48	8.51	10.72	11.45	12.88	14.32	17.15	18.6	20.0	21.40	22.9	MPH
50	8.94	11.2	11.9	13.4	14.9	17.9	19.4	20.8	22.3	23.85	MPH
52	9.3	11.68	12.4	13.95	15.5	18.5	20.2	21.65	23.2	24.9	MPH
54	9.65	12.1	12.9	14.5	16.2	19.3	20.9	22.5	24.1	25.9	MPH
56	10.0	12.5	13.4	15.0	16.7	20.0	21.7	23.4	25.0	26.75	MPH
58	10.36	12.95	13.82	15.55	17.3	20.7	22.5	24.2	25.9	27.6	MPH
60	10.75	13.4	14.3	16.1	17.9	21.4	23.25	25.0	26.8	28.7	MPH
62	11.1	13.85	14.8	16.6	18.5	22.2	24.0	25.85	27.7	29.6	MPH
64	11.43	14.3	15.3	17.2	19.1	22.9	24.8	26.7	28.6	30.5	MPH

66	11.8	14.64	15.65	17.7	19.7	23.6	25.6	27.5	29.6	31.5 MPH
68	12.12	15.2	16.3	18.2	20.3	24.3	26.4	28.4	30.5	32.45 MPH
70	12.51	15.65	16.7	18.75	21.0	25.0	27.1	29.2	31.3	33.4 MPH
72	12.87	16.1	17.2	19.3	21.5	25.7	27.9	30.0	32.2	34.4 MPH
74	13.2	16.58	17.7	19.8	22.1	26.55	28.7	30.9	33.0	35.3 MPH
76	13.6	17.0	18.1	20.4	22.7	27.2	29.4	31.7	34.0	36.3 MPH
78	13.9	17.4	18.6	20.9	23.4	27.9	30.2	32.6	34.8	37.2 MPH
80	14.3	17.9	19.1	21.45	23.9	28.6	31.0	33.3	35.8	38.2 MPH
82	14.62	18.35	19.5	22.0	24.5	29.4	31.8	34.2	36.65	39.1 MPH
84	15.0	18.8	20.0	22.6	25.1	30.0	32.6	35.0	37.6	40.0 MPH
86	15.4	19.2	20.55	23.0	25.75	30.7	33.4	35.9	38.4	41.1 MPH
88	15.7	19.7	21.0	23.6	26.3	31.5	34.15	36.8	39.3	42.0 MPH
90	16.1	20.2	21.5	24.2	27.0	32.2	34.8	37.5	40.2	43.0 MPH
92	16.44	20.6	22.0	24.65	27.45	32.8	35.6	38.3	41.3	43.9 MPH
94	16.8	21.0	22.45	25.2	28.1	33.6	36.4	39.2	42.0	44.9 MPH
96	17.15	21.5	22.95	25.75	28.7	34.3	37.2	40.0	42.8	45.8 MPH
98	17.5	21.9	23.4	26.2	29.25	35.0	38.0	40.8	43.8	46.7 MPH
100	17.9	22.4	23.9	26.8	29.95	35.75	38.8	41.7	44.8	47.8 MPH
102	18.2	22.8	24.4	27.3	30.45	36.55	39.6	42.6	45.7	48.8 MPH
104	18.6	23.25	24.85	27.9	31.0	37.25	40.4	43.4	46.7	49.6 MPH
106	18.9	23.7	25.3	28.4	31.3	37.9	41.3	44.2	47.5	50.6 MPH

Courtesy of CYCLO-PEDIA

Calibrated by Professor Paul R. "Pop" Kepner

appendix E

GEAR RATIO CHART FOR 27-INCH WHEELS

REAR GEAR	CHAIN WHEEL 54T	52T	50T	49T	48T	47T	46T	45T	44T	42T	40T	39T	38T	36T
13T	112.2	108.0	103.8	101.8	99.7	97.6	95.5	93.5	91.4	87.2	83.1	81.0	78.9	74.8
14T	104.1	100.3	96.4	94.5	92.6	90.6	88.7	86.8	84.9	81.0	77.1	75.2	73.3	69.4
15T	97.2	93.6	90.0	88.2	86.4	84.6	82.8	81.0	79.2	75.6	72.0	70.2	68.4	64.8
16T	91.1	87.8	84.4	82.7	81.0	79.3	77.6	75.9	74.2	70.9	67.5	65.8	64.1	60.8
17T	85.8	82.6	79.4	77.8	76.2	74.6	73.1	71.5	69.9	66.7	63.5	61.9	60.4	57.2
18T	81.0	78.0	75.0	73.5	72.0	70.5	69.0	67.5	66.0	63.0	60.0	58.5	57.0	54.0
19T	76.7	73.9	71.1	69.6	68.2	66.8	65.4	63.9	62.5	59.7	56.8	55.4	54.0	51.2
20T	72.9	70.2	67.5	66.2	64.8	63.4	62.1	60.8	59.4	56.7	54.0	52.6	51.3	48.6
21T	69.4	66.8	64.3	63.0	61.7	60.4	59.1	57.9	56.6	54.0	51.4	50.1	48.9	46.3
22T	66.3	63.8	61.4	60.1	58.9	57.7	56.5	55.2	54.0	51.5	49.1	47.9	46.6	44.2
23T	63.4	61.0	58.7	57.5	56.3	55.2	54.0	52.8	51.7	49.3	47.0	45.8	44.6	42.3
24T	60.8	58.5	56.2	55.1	54.0	52.9	51.8	50.6	49.5	47.2	45.0	43.9	42.8	40.5
25T	58.3	56.2	54.0	52.9	51.8	50.8	49.7	48.6	47.5	45.4	43.2	42.1	41.0	38.9
26T	56.1	54.0	51.9	50.9	49.8	48.8	47.8	46.7	45.7	43.6	41.5	40.5	39.5	37.4
27T	54.0	52.0	50.0	49.0	48.0	47.0	46.0	45.0	44.0	42.0	40.0	39.0	38.0	36.0
28T	52.1	50.1	48.2	47.2	46.3	45.3	44.4	43.4	42.4	40.5	38.6	37.6	36.6	34.7
30T	48.6	46.8	45.0	44.1	43.2	42.3	41.4	40.5	39.6	37.8	36.0	35.1	34.2	32.4
32T	45.6	43.9	42.2	41.3	40.5	39.7	38.8	38.0	37.1	35.4	33.8	32.9	32.1	30.4
34T	42.9	41.3	39.7	38.9	38.1	37.3	36.5	35.7	34.9	33.4	31.8	31.0	30.2	28.6

Courtesy of Shimano

INDEX